THE LIBRARY OF HOLOCAUST TESTIMONIES

From Thessaloniki to Auschwitz and Back

The Library of Holocaust Testimonies

Editors: Antony Polonsky, Martin Gilbert CBE, Aubrey Newman, Raphael F. Scharf, Ben Helfgott MBE

Under the auspices of the Yad Vashem Committee of the Board of Deputies of British Jews and the Centre for Holocaust Studies, University of Leicester

My Lost World by Sara Rosen
From Dachau to Dunkirk by Fred Pelican
Breathe Deeply, My Son by Henry Wermuth
My Private War by Jacob Gerstenfeld-Maltiel
A Cat Called Adolf by Trude Levi
An End to Childhood by Miriam Akavia
A Child Alone by Martha Blend
The Children Accuse by Maria Hochberg-Marianska and Noe Gruss
I Light a Candle by Gena Turgel
My Heart in a Suitcase by Anne L. Fox
Memoirs from Occupied Warsaw, 1942-1945 by Helena Szereszewska
Have You Seen My Little Sister? by Janina Fischler-Martinho
Surviving the Nazis, Exile and Siberia by Edith Sekules
Out of the Ghetto by Jack Klajman with Ed Klajman
From Thessaloniki to Auschwitz and Back by Erika Myriam Kounio Amariglio
Translated by Theresa Sundt
I Was No. 20832 at Auschwitz by Eva Tichauer
Translated by Colette Lévy and Nicki Rensten
My Child is Back! by Ursula Pawel
Wartime Experiences in Lithuania by Rivka Lozansky Bogomolnaya
Translated by Miriam Beckerman
Who Are You, Mr Grymek? by Natan Gross
Translated by William Brand
A Life Sentence of Memories by Issy Hahn, Foreword by Theo Richmond
An Englishman in Auschwitz by Leon Greenman
For Love of Life by Leah Iglinsky-Goodman
No Place to Run: The Story of David Gilbert by Tim Shortridge and Michael D. Frounfelter
A Little House on Mount Carmel by Alexandre Blumstein
From Germany to England Via the Kindertransports by Peter Prager
By a Twist of History: The Three Lives of a Polish Jew by Mietek Sieradzki
The Jews of Poznań by Zbigniew Pakula
Lessons in Fear by Henryk Vogler
To Live is to Forgive ... But Not Forget by Maja Abramowitch

From Thessaloniki to Auschwitz and Back

Memories of a Survivor from Thessaloniki

ERIKA MYRIAM KOUNIO AMARIGLIO

translated into English by
Theresa Sundt (neé Amariglio)
Thessaloniki 1998

VALLENTINE MITCHELL
LONDON • PORTLAND, OR

First published in 2000 in Great Britain by
VALLENTINE MITCHELL
Crown House, 47 Chase Side
London N14 5BP

and in the United States of America by
VALLENTINE MITCHELL
c/o ISBS, 5824 N. E. Hassalo Street
Portland, Oregon 97213-3644

Website: www.vmbooks.com

British Library Cataloguing in Publication Data
Amariglio, Erika Myriam Kounio
From Thessaloniki to Auschwitz and back: memories of a survivor from Thessaloniki. – (The library of Holocaust testimonies)
1. Amariglio, Erika Myriam Kounio 2. Holocaust, Jewish (1939–1945) – Personal narratives 3. Auschwitz (Concentration camp) 4. Thessaloniki (Greece) – History
I. Title
940.5'318'092
ISBN 0-85303-390-0
ISSN 1363-3759

Library of Congress Cataloging-in-Publication Data
Kounio-Amariglio, Erika, 1926–
[Penenta chronia meta – English]
From Thessaloniki to Auschwitz and back: memories of a survivor from Thessaloniki/Erikah Myriam Kounio Amariglio.
p. cm.
ISBN 0-85303-390-0 (pbk.)
1. Kounio-Amariglio, Erika, 1926– 2. Jews – Persecutions – Greece.
3. Holocaust, Jewish (1939–1945) – Greece – Personal narratives. 4. Greece – Ethnic relations. I. Title.

DS135.G73 K68413 2000
940.5'318'092–dc21
[B] 00-025900

Printed and bound in Great Britain by
The Cromwell Press, Trowbridge, Wiltshire

Contents

List of Illustrations

Biographical Note

Erika Myriam Kounio Amariglio was born in Thessaloniki. In March 1943 she and her family were among 2,800 people who were deported with the first transport to Auschwitz extermination camp. She remained there for two-and-a-half years. Due to her knowledge of German, she worked as a scribe in the camp's Gestapo office. After the war, she returned to Greece and married. In 1964 she began a career in Tupperware which lasted 21 years. Since her retirement she has done voluntary work and fundraising for Israel and traveled with her husband. The book has previously appeared in Greek, German, French and Serbian editions and a Hebrew edition was published in April 1999.

The Library of Holocaust Testimonies

It is greatly to the credit of Frank Cass that this series of survivors' testimonies is being published in Britain. The need for such a series has long been apparent here, where many survivors made their homes.

Since the end of the war in 1945 the terrible events of the Nazi destruction of European Jewry have cast a pall over our time. Six million Jews were murdered within a short period; the few survivors have had to carry in their memories whatever remains of the knowledge of Jewish life in more than a dozen countries, in several thousand towns, in tens of thousands of villages, and in innumerable families. The precious gift of recollection has been the sole memorial for millions of people whose lives were suddenly and brutally cut off.

For many years, individual survivors have published their testimonies. But many more have been reluctant to do so, often because they could not believe that they would find a publisher for their efforts.

In my own work over the past two decades, I have been approached by many survivors who had set down their memories in writing, but who did not know how to have them published. I realized what a considerable emotional strain the writing down of such hellish memories had been. I also realized, as I read many dozens of such accounts, how important each account was, in its own way, in recounting aspects of the story that had not been told before, and adding to our understanding of the wide range of human suffering, struggle and aspiration.

With so many people and so many places involved, including many hundreds of camps, it was inevitable that the historians and students of the Holocaust should find it difficult at times to grasp the scale and range of the events. The publication of memoirs is therefore an indispensable part of the extension of knowledge, and of public awareness of the crimes that had been committed against a whole people.

Martin Gilbert
Merton College, Oxford

Acknowledgements

I would like to thank Robin Sundt, Costas Lambrianidis and James Brice for their precious help with the translation and editing of the English edition.

But most of all, I would like to thank my beloved daughter, Theresa, who made the original translation. She relived my experiences day after day for half a year, to make sure that the feeling of the original Greek is accurately reflected in a different language. Her help was invaluable, not only for the completion of the English version, but also because it led to a special warm relationship being built between us.

Prologue

In the course of the years many people urged me to write down my experiences in the concentration camps. My answer was always spontaneous and always the same: 'Why should I write about events that so many others have already described, especially so many important people …' I said this over and over, and I thoroughly believed it.

The years passed, and many things happened. Today, half a century later, we hear more and more people saying that the Holocaust never happened, that it was not as tragic as people describe it, that it was not six million Jews who were killed, as if there were fewer victims and it was not human beings like you and I who died … and 'after all,' certain people say 'the Second World War had so many more victims. So many thousands of soldiers, for one thing, so many hundreds of women and children killed by bombs, hunger and hardship. So many thousands fought and died in the resistance.'

But the six million did nothing more than to be born of the wrong womb.

These stories are not just survivors' tales, there is irrefutable proof in the camp archives confirming that there were gas chambers and crematoria – 'ovens', the testimonies of survivors and the documents, meticulously detailed lists the Germans kept of everything that happened in the camps day-in, day-out; detailed documentation of orders and decisions that the commanders made; records of the experiments they made on human beings; descriptions SS officers themselves made, i.e., the diary of the camp administrator, Rudolf Hoess … and many others; pictures the SS put in their private albums and in their archives; films the Nazis made that still survive in various museums.

Year after year, I hear that more and more people are denying and distorting the truth about the Holocaust.

My remaining years are growing shorter all the time, and

soon my contemporaries and I will no longer be among the living. The last of the witnesses to the Holocaust will some day be gone.

Fifty years later, I too now feel a need to write my own testimony and to memorialize my cousins, my relatives, my three beloved friends and classmates, Dorin Kovo, Rita Saltiel and May Benrubi, who went through the first selection and were admitted to the camps, not in order to survive, but to live as long as they could endure the hardship, the forced labor and the hunger, and the friends I met and loved so much inside the concentration camps who did not survive.

Fifty years later everything is still vivid in my memory. Although the pain has dulled, my wonder and astonishment grows steadily, confronted by the inconceivable, by something the human soul cannot accept no matter what the rationale, the justification: how is it possible that they deceived so many millions of people with such skill and psychological subtlety? How were they able to conceive of and operate such an efficient machine of death? Why didn't the people living near the different camps, who knew what was happening inside, do anything? How? How? Why?

Many years passed, and I could not recount or talk about the two-and-a-half years I spent in the concentration camps where I found myself without having done anything to deserve this outrage. I was born Jewish, only that …

One day a door suddenly opened in my mind. Why not? So I started to write down my own memories. Many times I became discouraged – and there were many of these times – but each time Franpiski Abazopoulou, Rika Benveniste and my husband were always at my side to offer so much understanding and encouragement. For that I thank them.

Erika Myriam Kounio Amariglio

Preface

When my mother's book was first published, 50 years after the liberation, it was a revelation to me. We were brought up in the shadow of the concentration camp, closely sheltered by my mother's profound love and solicitude for us. We were nurtured with the powerful optimism and thirst for life of a survivor and the deep and desperate sadness of a person who has seen evil eye-to-eye. But it was only when my mother wrote down her experiences that I first understood the magnitude of her trauma and the anxiety that years of bottling it up had caused her.

When her book was first published (in Greek), my eldest son Charles was 16 years old – the same age as my mother when she was transported to Auschwitz. There were times when reading and later translating thc book that I found myself putting Charles in her place, trying to see through his mind's eye and crying for him and for my mother as a young innocent girl of the same age. At times the juxtaposition of these two people, both so dear to me, made me so anxious that I had to force myself out of the nightmare and back into the present. Then I would run to hug and kiss an astonished Charles and call my mother in Greece on the telephone just to say 'Hello!'

When I was translating the book, I had to work carefully, weighing every single word and phrase of the text – no skimming through the painful sections, I had to concentrate on every word. I cried and mourned for the people who suffered, who were tortured, who died, who lost forever the sunshine in their hearts. It was a nine-month-long memorial service to the victims of the Holocaust. A sad and burdensome winter. I wished the translation to be finished, dreading the ghosts waiting for me on the dining room table to tell me their frightening stories. I could easily understand why people did not want to listen to the survivors when they came out of the camps. Their stories were too horrifying to bear in the difficult years after the war.

Fifty years later the last of the survivors are being encouraged to talk about the Holocaust so that people will know about it. There are even those who claim that the systematic extermination of the Jews never happened. The sad thing is that the Holocaust did happen, as did many 'smaller' Holocausts, going on even at this very moment. Fifty years after the liberation, the Serbs, Croats, Bosnians and Kosovans are at each other's throats because of their ethnic origins. I heard a young woman who escaped from Croatia interviewed on the radio: 'They killed my parents, my brothers, my aunts and uncles and they destroyed our house just because we are Croatian.' My mother asks the troubling question in this book of why she and her relatives were persecuted when their only crime was to be Jewish. Sadly, history has a habit of repeating itself over and over again. Human nature can be absolutely magnificent – or totally destructive.

My translation stays as close to the original Greek text as possible; I have tried to endow it with a feeling of the everyday language my mother uses in her book. Hopefully the text will evoke some of the freshness of her account as seen through the eyes of a 16-year-old.

I wish to thank my mother for giving us in writing such an important part of herself to treasure forever and for our children and grandchildren. I also thank her for all her efforts and struggles to make my brother and me into decent human beings.

Thank you mama, I love you very much.

Theresa Sundt (née Amariglio)*
Surrey, England, January 1998

* The author's daughter and translater of this English version.

Glossary

Appell	roll call.
Aussenkommando	labor detachment working outside.
Blockälteste	head of (accommodation) block (not SS).
'Canada'-Kommando	labor detachment dealing with incomers' possessions.
Kapo	head of workforce.
Kommando	labor detachment/workforce.
Politische Abteilung (PA)	office of the camp, Gestapo, dealing with all administration matters.
Revier	sick-bay.
Reichssicherheitschauptamt (RSHA)	Nazi Security Department.
Sonderbehandlung (SB)	'special treatment': written by the names of those killed in the gas chambers.
Schuh-Kommando	workforce who mended shoes.
Schupo	policeman.
Sonderkommando (SDK)	workforce attached to the crematoria.
Union-Werke-Kommando	munitions workforce.

To the memory of the 23 members of my family who perished in Birkenau concentration camp and to my beloved friends and classmates, Dorin Kovo, May Benrubi and Rita Saltiel, who perished together with them.

1 • *A Happy Childhood in Thessaloniki*

In 1924 my father, Salvator Kounio, then twenty-four, already had a small shop where he sold photographic equipment. Industrious and eager to learn, he acquired many good customers right from the start. He supplied all the street photographers that came to his shop with photographic paper and anything else they needed for their work. They admired and respected him greatly, because he was always there to advise and help them to become more successful. Many of them later opened their own photo shops, and their friendship with my father continued to grow.

Some of them, the younger ones, are still alive. They remember him and still speak fondly of him. One of these is Jannis Kiriakidis, the well-known photojournalist from Thessaloniki – who doesn't know of him in this city? Every time he meets me and has a few minutes to spare, he tells me how much Salvator Kounio helped him to get started in his own business.

In those days my father used to import photographic paper from Germany, and every year he visited the exhibition in Leipzig, the biggest photographic exhibition in Europe at that time. In 1924, through a mutual friend, he met Hella Loevy, a third-year medical student at the University of Leipzig. They fell in love at first sight, and my mother decided to abandon her studies and follow him to Greece.

Her father was a famous architect and engineer who lived in Karlsbad – then in Austro-Hungary, but later to become 'Karlovi-vari' in Czechoslovakia, now the Czech Republic. Her mother, Theresa, was a beautiful and cultured Viennese lady. They were not at all enthusiastic about their only daughter's decision. But their 18-year-old daughter, as stubborn and strong-willed then as she has been ever since, managed to convince them, and in June 1925 they were married in Karlsbad.

Meanwhile our house was built in one of the most beautiful areas of Thessaloniki, the 'Rural District', extending from the White Tower to Depo. Large and small houses, two or three storeys high with large gardens, dotted the area. My grandfather designed the house and supervised its construction. My father's concern was to make it a comfortable house with every amenity. He wanted his young bride, who had sacrificed her studies and her whole lifestyle for his sake, to feel comfortable and at ease at any cost.

Mother, brought up in Vienna and Karlsbad in Austro-Hungary and already a third-year student at the University of Leipzig, suddenly found herself in a world totally different from her previous one. In the 1920s Thessaloniki was really unlike the rest of Europe. She needed a lot of inner strength to overcome the barrier of being a 'foreigner', as everybody called her – even her friends and relatives – and to be accepted by Thessalonikian society. A year later, at the end of March 1926, in that same house, I was born – in those days children were born at home, not in a hospital.

Our house in Koromila Street was built by the sea. Together with two neighboring houses, to the left and the right of ours, and the gardens of the Lycée Français, later the Fifth Public High School, lined the shore of a small bay.

How small our house looked squeezed in between the two bigger houses, Vozios' on our left and Polat's on our right. Both had three floors and a tower with a steep conical roof. I imagined them to be two sentinels protecting our house, small as it was. It was not really small at all, with four bedrooms upstairs and a large bathroom. Downstairs there was a dining room, sitting room and a large kitchen. A most beautiful staircase led upstairs to the bedrooms. How many times my brother and I slid down the solid banister! Underneath in the

Erika's parents' house in Saloniki, 1960.

basement was the coal cellar and the wood cellar, always tightly packed with logs neatly stacked, one on top of the other. This served as our hiding place when we played hide-and-seek.

On the ground floor, covering the whole length of the house, there was a wide veranda. In the middle of the veranda wide marble steps led into the backyard. The yard was covered with a layer of white pebbles, and every year father would bring in fresh pebbles to fill the gaps.

The yard ended with a small, one-meter-high wall, then there was a gap of about four meters between the wall and a breakwater holding back the sea. To reinforce the breakwater, the gap was filled with large boulders piled randomly to fill the space.

The sea flowed through gaps in the breakwater, foaming in amongst the boulders. Big and little crabs took shelter between the stones, and I can still hear the sea splashing, caressing the stones when the strong north wind (*Vardaris*) wasn't blowing. Part of the left side of the boulders was covered with cement, forming a platform that connected the breakwater to the little wall. Four small steps led up from the yard to the platform. Two large pieces of inverted 'L'-shaped iron beams with pulleys on the ends on the seaward side of the platform were used to raise our little white boat, *The Lorelei*. A very strong, solid wooden ladder with big iron hand grips extended down the side of the breakwater into the sea.

That was where we used to go swimming in the sea. The grown-ups climbed up and down the ladder with dignity, while we children constantly jumped in and out of the water. The seabed was covered with big stones, and it was difficult to stand up. Very few of the grown-ups went barefoot; they were afraid of the crabs, mussels and sea urchins, but we children weren't bothered by them.

I had two or three special boulders of my own, and there I would stand fearlessly. I remember the sailboats, bringing fresh gravel for the yard, that tied up to the breakwater. The holds of the boats were full of stones which they shoveled into sacks. Then the '*Hamals*', carriers, carried the sacks on their backs and emptied them into our yard. We watched this procedure with great interest, together with all the neighborhood children, just as we did when they went to unload gravel for our neighbors' yards.

From our breakwater we also embarked on the big boat

that came to pick us up together with my parents' friends and take us to Ai-Jannis on Pilion – there was no other way to get to Ai-Jannis in those days. The trip must have lasted one or two days, because I remember that we used to spread blankets and pillows in the hold so that we could sleep there. The blankets and the household goods we brought with us were used during our stay there. Ai-Jannis was isolated and remote then; there were no hotels as there are today. Only the first YMCA camping place was already there. Then gradually this beautiful and secluded place began to become known.

At the edges of the breakwater, right and left, there were iron barriers, a big bow with sharp protruding spikes. The barrier that separated us from our neighbor on the left was bigger (and made of thicker iron bars) than the one on the right. The one on the right was smaller and made of thinner iron bars, more of a decoration than a barrier. Mr Vozios had built a tall, 2-meter-high wall that separated our two houses along the length of the platform, but near the breakwater it was only just over a meter high. On top of the wall he had arranged pieces of broken bottle glass, stuck into the cement, so that nobody would jump over and get inside.

Our neighbor took these precautions because inside the breakwater in front of his house he had built a small artificial pool: 'Vozios' Pool', as we used to call it. He had set up a very clever system to trap fish: they entered through openings in the breakwater that were three to four times larger than ours. On the openings in the breakwater he installed iron sluice gates that went up and down. He lifted the gates and let the fish in. At a certain time of the day he would close the gates again, trapping the fish that had swum in. Most of them were small mullet, sea bream and others. Now and then sole would also come in – easy prey for poachers.

My brother, a year younger than I, always had a great passion for fishing. He would get up at dawn to prepare bait for mullet – bread and cheese, well kneaded together – and fish for hours. Many times I sat and fished with him for a while, but the fish preferred his bait most of the time. The cheese and bread we prepared as bait was very tasty, not only for the fish, but also for us as well. I always made more than we needed so that I too could 'nibble' on this delicious bait.

One of our greatest delights was to hunt for and catch the big crabs that used to hide among the rocks. Across the length of the breakwater there was a small ledge at sea level. This little wall was completely covered by mussels that hung like bunches of grapes all the way down into the depths of the water.

Many times the crabs relaxed their guard too much and climbed up on the ledge to sunbathe. We had both acquired great skill in catching these crabs and pinning down their claws. I was not as good as my brother because I was scared of the claws, but he was an expert. We placed a can full of water next to us, and as soon as we caught some crabs we threw them in. Our joy was great and our triumphant cries echoed in the air whenever we caught big crabs, 'grabs' as we called them: 'I have him, I have him, what a "grab",' my brother would shout.

The best 'grabs' we brought to my mother, who boiled them, and then we ate them. I cannot recollect eating tastier seafood than those 'grabs', all bright-red from boiling. I was always careful not to break the shells. They were so beautiful that I saved them. Usually our friends and neighbors accompanied us on these expeditions.

The platform that connected the inside of the wall with the breakwater was ideal for adults to sunbathe and for us children to leap into the sea. Running from one end to the other and taking a big jump, we competed to see who could leap the farthest.

We also had a 'beauty' in our neighborhood – a good friend and really a very beautiful girl. She came every day and spent hours getting a good tan and scolded us ever so often for spraying her with water when we jumped in. Not that it made any difference to us …

My father had built a little wooden hut – we called it the

'barrack' – painted in a charming green color, which made it easier for friends to undress undisturbed and leave their clothes while swimming.

Our great joy was to sit on the roof of the hut at sunset with a big loaf of bread with cheese in the middle and gaze at the sea and the sky, aglow with many different colors in the setting sun.

Our platform, I remember, was full of people, in contrast to our neighbor's, who wouldn't allow any 'strangers' to use his.

Despite the iron railings and his wall topped with broken glass, children from the neighborhood would go into his garden and fish for his trapped fish. The minute he became aware of it he ran out with a stick yelling at them, 'Little rascals, I will show you now.' The children thoroughly enjoyed this, and so did we – and of course at the first opportunity they crossed the wall again.

Opposite our house, and across from Mr Polat's breakwater, the road ended in a jetty. Thus in front of our house and our neighbors' a little bay was formed, closed on three sides and open to the sea. The water was shallow there with no stones, only sand: a little paradise for mothers and their little ones and anyone who couldn't swim too far.

During the summer months, from early in the morning till late in the afternoon, laughter and children's voices echoed in the air, together with the splashes which rang out when we leapt in.

There, in that 'lagoon', old 'Uncle' Gregorius moored his boat. We all loved him, but we were also afraid of him. How much he cared for his boat! It was painted brilliant white with a light blue-and-red band around the top. The keel, painted dark red, gave a happy touch to the boat. The bow, of plain wood, very well polished, looked excessively luxurious. He often put a flower on the stern, and he always hung the traditional Mayday wreath on it. On the seats there were embroidered cushions. Each had its own design stitched with lively colors in backstitch. One depicted a mermaid emerging from the sea. Another was decorated with colorful flowers, butterflies and little birds. On the middle cushion, which was the largest, the name of the boat was embroidered with the motto: 'Move forward and God will provide.'

Naturally these were the good, the formal cushions that he used on Sundays and holidays when he took families for rides. That is when he also set up a small white canopy with bobbles on the sides and embroidered with red thread to protect his passengers from the burning sun. His everyday cushions were simple, made from calico.

When he was sober during the week, and if he felt in the mood, he would fish. He used to talk to us then and often gave us advice on how to fish better. I loved listening to him and looking at his smiling blue eyes and big mustache, rising and falling as he talked. I often wondered how he could eat. Didn't his mustache get in the way?

But when we swam too close to his boat and frightened his fish away, or when we splashed his 'good' cushions while he was waiting for customers, his rage came straight down from the heavens. We had to disappear. And he was right. His boat was like a jewel when it was all decked out. Brilliant white, with its canopy, the good cushions and himself shining in his spotlessly clean clothes and indispensable straw hat. He waited, oars in hand. His mustache could hardly hide his smile of happiness. He was an unforgettable spectacle, old Gregorius with his boat crossing the sea up and down in front of our house.

I remember one Sunday when Vozios' family were all dressed up in their best clothes ready for an 'excursion' in old Gregorius' boat. My brother and I with two of our friends were watching from our platform as the boat embarked.

I remember the ladies, beautifully attired. They wore lovely hats and were holding small handbags. The three girls, all very pretty, wore their hair in long curls. Thalia especially, who was my age, was absolutely stunning, with her long blonde hair all in curls. Good old Gregorius was standing on the boat holding the gunnel with one hand and helping people climb in with the other hand. Just like an admiral he was, giving out commands on how to sit, so that the boat would balance. With a push he left the breakwater and slowly started rowing.

They hadn't gone far when one of the passengers clumsily stood up. And there was the boat, tilting dangerously, Gregorius said something, then another person stood up. The boat tilted and all of them fell into the water. We watched and giggled. The ladies' dainty hats floated ingloriously on the waves. The flower that old Gregorius had put on the stern also floated proudly, and Thalia's gorgeous curls were gone. The ahs and ohs echoed in our ears. Fortunately they were all good swimmers and got out of the water safely.

We were secretly pleased at Mr Vozios' mishap. We were angry and fed up with him, because he always found reasons to be mad at us. It might have been because we were too noisy during his siesta, when he was asleep but not us, or because somebody opened the breakwater gates and let the trapped fish out, or for any other mischief. We were always to blame.

I remember that he always used to place the watermelon of the day in a wooden washtub in the basement of his house, which was also the washroom, letting the tap run to cool it. He let the water drip over the melon so it was just cool enough by lunch-time, ready to eat. We did not yet have refrigerators, and his ice-box was not big enough to accommodate 'the bomb' that his big family required.

One day Thalia called us to examine a huge oblong watermelon that looked very heavy. 'Impossible to lift,' she said. Then my brother beat his breast with his fists and exclaimed, 'I'm a muscle man,' and tried to show off his strength.

'I shall lift it,' he proclaimed.

Thalia egged him on, 'You can't do it, you can't do it!'

The truth was that he could not do it; he was a very weak boy, but very stubborn. There were four or five children there, and 'muscle man' wanted to show off. With an enormous effort he lifted the watermelon with his thin arms, carried it to the door, around ten meters away, and turned back to return it to the washtub. But his strength was exhausted, and in his effort to put it back in the washtub, it slipped through his hands and shattered with a loud CRASH on the floor.

We all stared at the bright chunks of red watermelon scattered on the ground, unable to utter a word, all except Thalia, who permitted a loud 'Oh!' to escape from her lips.

The silence didn't last long. One of the children bent down and picked up a piece, 'My, my, how tasty!' Without a second thought we all, including Thalia, pounced on the melon and started to eat with great gusto. After that we picked up the pieces of rind, cleaned the place as best we could and left. We spent all morning in anxious fear of how Vozios would react when he found out what we had done. It is easy to imagine what happened then. We heard his booming voice. Like 'good little children' we huddled quietly in a corner of our veranda.

When father came back at lunch-time, with lowered heads we went to tell him about our 'deed'. I don't remember him being angry with us, although I am sure he must have said something to us. He went straight to Vozios and paid for the watermelon. I remember that my brother didn't mention his being a 'muscle man' again for a long time afterward.

I suspect that our neighbor did not forget that 'historical watermelon', the best of that year, for a long time. Most of the time, when he was mad at us he had a right to be, but we didn't care. Even his misadventures seemed very funny to us.

Summer began officially on St Constantine's day (21 May), but we started swimming as soon as the weather permitted. We spent all day by the sea, fishing, in our boat, swimming or holding swimming competitions and contests to see who could dive the best.

A bit farther away from our house, on the other side of the jetty, was the Greco's house. It was a very beautiful, large house, located close to the water with a lovely wide breakwater, private saltwater pond and many large platforms.

It was a fair distance from our house, and we loved swimming there.

Half way through each summer our sea literally teemed with people. One could see ladies swimming while holding on to big inflatable cushions on which they rested their heads as they kicked their legs. The cushions were made of calico, a thick fabric that kept the water out when it was wet. In order to inflate them more easily, they sewed wooden bobbins on the edges – and blocked the holes with a wooden peg or well-chewed piece of chewing gum! The cushions floated like small crowns of foam. I was delighted when I was allowed to borrow one from my neighbor and swim with it. My mother wouldn't permit us to have one: she said: 'The cushions are for people who don't know how to swim!'

During the summer we took our meals on the veranda, morning, noon and evening, and we enjoyed the lovely view of the sea, in which colors and shapes changed constantly as the sun moved across the sky.

The boats sailing from the city to Perea, Baxe and Agia Triada ornamented the sea. One of our games was to guess which boat was passing by; was it *Lefki*, *Alekos*, *Triglia*, *Poseidon* or some other one.

Alas, if the north wind (*Vardaris*) blew up suddenly, these normally enjoyable trips became a torture. The trips were canceled because they were too dangerous. We heard many times that *Triglia* – and it usually was *Triglia* – had sunk again off the Perea bridge. In the evenings when the boats returned their lights were lit up, and they looked like jewelry with precious stones glittering over the sea as they approached the pier in the city.

From our veranda we could see in the distance the town and the upper town. When the sun set, its rays often fell on the panes of windows. The orange color of the sunset made the windows light up. Later, when night came, Thessaloniki emerged like a multi-colored brooch decorated with colorful gems. How much I loved to sit there alone and watch my beautiful town.

Smaller ships crossed the stretch between the city and Luxembourg, very close to our house. Luxembourg was the most popular entertainment center in those days, and it was in full swing. Many big-name entertainers sang or brought their bands there. One summer the very famous Eduardo Bianco came with his orchestra. The center teemed with people every evening.

I remember my parents dressing up in great excitement in order to go and dance to Bianco's passionate tangos. It was one of the few times that I saw my father so excited about anything. He invited Bianco to our house and the latter gave my father sheet music to all his songs and also music for my mother to play on the piano. The dedication he wrote on them was so warm that my father showed it to me, full of pride.

As the center was by the seaside, in the evening boats full of people plied up and down, while their passengers enjoyed the beautiful melodies in the sweet summer nights.

Our bedroom faced Koromila Street, and with the shutters open, lying in our beds, we could hear the music filling the night, the air smelling of jasmine and musk. At other times we could hear wandering troubadours serenading one of the 'belles' of the neighborhood. Our neighbor's eldest daughter, Gloria, was very much sought after, and our street was very popular among the troubadours, to my great delight. I very much loved to hear their songs, and I sang with them and dreamed of the time when I would come of age and they would come to sing for me as well!

Sometimes I could also hear the odd splash of a bucket of water thrown on them to make them stop singing. Often the singers were accompanied on guitars, and their songs sounded even more beautiful then. Until late autumn we could hear them in the evenings, wandering around our narrow streets and singing 'Your Eyes' or 'The Nightingale Told Me' and many other songs.

Sunsets in the Gulf of Thessaloniki are well known for their unique beauty. My mother taught me how to tell from the color of the sunset if there will be a north wind, or if we would have another beautiful day. When the horizon was bright red, we knew it would be windy.

In those days the north wind '*Vardaris*' – the strong wind that came from the River Axios – regulated our lives (due to building it is less apparent now). The sea swelled and big waves crashed against the breakwater. Drops of salt water splashed against the windows of our house. We could not sit on the veranda then. The wind raised a thin cloud of dust that 'prickled' our faces. It would last, according to the fishermen, 24 hours or from three days to a week.

The sea became deserted then. Old Gregorius pulled his boat on to the shore. Fishing was out, and only very brave souls dared to go swimming. Fortunately my mother allowed us to swim, but only when she herself was present. We jumped from the platform as far as we could, because the big waves carried us all the way back to the breakwater. What a great pleasure to ride on the waves!

In order to get out of the water, we had to go next door to Mrs Olga's house, where the water was shallow.

When the north wind blew, it was an opportunity for us to play all the regular neighborhood games – hide-and-seek, *beekos*, *tsilika-tsoma-ka*, and for the girls hopscotch and jacks. We each had our five round pebbles and for hopscotch our very own stones.

The wind was hard on our houses. It came whistling into them through the cracks. There was a constant buzz in my ears from the waves crashing against the breakwater. Out in the street, many a time we had to lean against the wind so that we wouldn't fall down. Everything that wasn't fastened down blew around with the wind. Pots were knocked over, windows were broken, shutters banged, bags and newspapers whirled about in the wind.

During the summer, every afternoon when father went to work, we accompanied him to the tram stop, walking across Koromila Street up to Vasilissis Olga Avenue. It was a tradition and a ritual to stop at the Ivi Patisserie to eat the best ice cream in Thessaloniki! We joyfully looked forward to it every day. Ritza, my best friend, followed the same routine when she strolled with her father. It was part of our summer life until the war in 1940.

Another typical feature of our neighborhood was Phaedon's motorbike. In those days this was a rare sight. A blond rider in a black leather jacket, Phaedon rode up and down the streets of our neighborhood, and we all went out to see him and to admire him as soon as we heard the sound of his engine from far away.

Our school, the Institute Zachariadis, was close to home. We walked there together with Ritza; either she picked me up, or I picked her up. We met with other schoolmates on the way there. How much we had to tell each other! So much news gathered since the day before. Laughing and giggling we arrived at school just before the bell rang. Often we met boys from our class: Kostas Labrianidis, Giorgos Nikolaidis, Loenidas, Andreas, Jannis Kechayas. With a pointed air of indifference we paid little attention to them.

Together with the start of the school year, we celebrated the most important Jewish holiday, Yom Kippur. None of the Jewish children went to school that day. Many children skipped classes. On that special day our teachers never taught anything terribly important.

I remember how impressed I was by that holiday when my father explained its meaning for the first time. 'It is a day of great repentance and of fasting,' he said to me. Which means? 'It is a day when you do nothing except recollect your deeds throughout the past year: if you did wrong, if you lied, if you offended a friend, if you were arrogant! You fast all day and you pray to God, asking him to forgive you and ask forgiveness of the people you have been unjust to. We go to the synagogue where we all pray and in the evening, at the conclusion of the holiday, the whole family gathers together to start a new year with love and unity and resolve to do the best that is humanly possible in the new year.'

Yom Kippur, and in the springtime, Passover, was what made us sense the religious differences between us and our Christian friends. But this did not affect our relationships. We never felt different, we were all the same and we all believed in the same God.

Two or three times a year, I remember my parents taking us to the Aboav Orphanage on Fleming Street. There was a large hall for weddings, engagements and memorial services. That was where my family, which was pretty big – my father had six brothers and sisters – gathered, and we held an annual memorial service for one of our relatives. I remember that when the service was over my brother and I each took a tray of pastries and treated the orphans to sweets. I never felt too good when I thought of how many things we had, my brother and I, and how much these children were missing. These 'memorials' were another opportunity for the family to gather together at times other than Yom Kippur and Passover.

I will always have pleasant memories of my grandmother Myriam and my grandfather Mosche. On holidays grandmother, or better – 'nona' – as we used to call her, put on her traditional outfit, that of a Sephardic Jew. White blouse embroidered with very small pearls, long skirt with a decorative apron tied in a bow at the front. On top she had a kind of coat called a *kofia* made of thick satin of an electric blue color and trimmed all around with fur. On her head she wore a scarf covering her forehead, beautifully stitched with designs and small pearls. How much I loved to look at her dressed like that. She liked to hide her hands under her apron.

Many times I wanted to caress her *kofia* fur, but I never dared to. Maybe because I could not communicate that well with my nona. My nona's Greek was very poor, because her language was Ladino (a mixture of Greek and Spanish) which we never spoke at home. We spoke our mother's native language, German, and my father's, Greek.

My grandfather – my 'nono' – with his big beard and very gentle face, always had something good to tell us. We spoke Greek with him, and even today I feel the warmth of his hand holding mine.

Grandfather Ernst Lőwy with Erika and Heinz, 1933.

From right to left: Grandmother Theresa Lőwy, Erika, Heinz and Grandmother Myriam Kounio, 1936.

Of course I also had another grandfather, named Ernst, and another grandmother, named Theresa, mother's parents. They didn't live with us, but rather in Karlsbad.

Every summer we used to stay with them for several weeks. We enjoyed these trips to Karlsbad so much that we looked forward to them throughout the year.

In those days it was really a long trip. We took the train, on which we slept for two nights until we arrived in Prague. There were no flights, and the trains were not as fast as today. I remember how luxurious our compartment seemed and how well we were looked after by the attendants. We loved sleeping in our beds with white starched sheets, and even more we loved going to the restaurant car, where there were little table lamps on the tables with pretty shades.

Grandpa and grandma waited for us full of anticipation. Grandfather held a decorative walking stick in his hand, tall, proud, with his hat on his bald head and his big mustache in the style of Kaiser Franz Joseph.

He was very fashionable and reserved. Only his eyes beamed. My grandmother, most beautiful – at least in my own eyes – with her hat on one side of her well-groomed hair, always wore smart dresses with her gloves and her little handbag. She opened her arms wide to embrace and hold me tight.

It was a completely different world from the one we left behind in Greece. Here everything was more elegant and proper; ladies strolled on the streets wearing beautiful hats and outfits, and the gentlemen, with their walking sticks and hats, looked very imposing.

I loved it when grandmother took us for a walk on the town square, where hot water bubbled up from hot springs.

In the center of the square was a great hot spring that blew scalding water high into the air. My grandmother said the water was expelled continuously with such force that it reached a height of a hundred meters and was 100 degrees centigrade. It was medicinal water, good for relieving many disorders, which is why Karlsbad was one of the best-known and most popular spas.

People strolled about holding a special cup in their hands, sipping *Sprudelwasser* (sparkling water) and listening to music. The town's municipal orchestra played every afternoon for the strollers. All around there were lovely lawns and flower beds. Under beautiful awnings there were tables and chairs offering rest, coffee, drinks or cake to the strolling guests. I felt as if I were in the midst of a beautiful fairy tale.

Then it was time for the biggest pleasure of the day – we went to a wonderful patisserie where we could choose anything we wanted, pastry or ice cream.

It was particularly special when we went to the luxurious patisserie at the Hotel Pupp. Its luxury and patrons totally fascinated me.

The days went by rapidly, as each day my grandparents planned something special to entertain us. The last time we went there was in 1937. I was already eleven, and I have the best memories from that particular summer. I watched with great fascination my grandmother's friends holding their parasols, some open, some closed. The gentlemen, with elegant gestures, took off their hats to greet any passing acquaintance and gracefully bowed quite low to the ground.

I loved talking to my grandmother and helping her with her chores.

That summer seemed to go by very rapidly, and I bid farewell to them at the station with a heavy heart. But when we returned home, old and new joys were awaiting us. It was still summer, and our friends were waiting for us. The sea was there as well, as always clear, blue and tempting.

In October we returned to school. I was in my fifth year, the next year would be my sixth year.

In 1938 another new year began. What would this year bring? I was looking forward to advancing to the sixth class. I felt grown up already. In between our games and our nonchalance, I heard troubled discussions by my parents. Hitler's name was often mentioned. They listened anxiously to the news from Germany and to the BBC. They talked about the German Jews in a very anxious tone of voice.

I picked up bits and pieces of their conversations without being able to understand very much. I could just feel a heavy cloud spreading over us.

'We are not going to Karlsbad this summer,' my mother told us, 'but don't you worry, grandfather and grandmother will come to us, to stay with us for ever and ever.'

That year my father promised to take me to Athens. My wish would finally come true. I would visit the Acropolis and I would visit the offices of *Diaplasis* (which means 'Children's Education' or 'Children's Life').

Diaplasis was my favorite magazine, and I was a faithful subscriber and keen contributor. I often took part in competitions under two different pen names – a known one, 'Goldfinch' and a secret one, 'Chatterbox'. I acquired many pen-pals throughout Greece through the magazine, and I always had something to contribute to its classified section.

Every Thursday I waited impatiently for the postman to deliver my beloved magazine! I wanted to meet 'Anania', the humor columnist in person, and to kiss 'Phaedon' – another writer who always ended his articles with the words, 'I kiss you, Phaedon.' I had created such a beautiful picture in my mind of *Diaplasis*' offices and staff. I could hardly wait for the day of our departure. My visit there would be *the* event of the year.

Athens was such a beautiful city in those days. Full of reverence I went up to the Acropolis, and full of awe I stood in front of the Kariatids. I was so happy to walk on the 'sacred mount', and I felt so small in front of the Parthenon. It was really one of the big days in my life.

The next morning my father brought me to the offices of *Diaplasis* for our visit. What a letdown! A narrow road and a narrow door (not at all imposing) that just had a sign 'Children's *Diaplasis*' – not even in gold letters.

An overturned dustbin stood in front of it, and as we opened the door a huge black cat jumped out. The office on the first floor was extremely simple, a bit on the dusty side and rather deserted. After a while a cleaning lady came out to tell us that nobody was there. How dreadful I felt. Was this the office after all? But where were Anania and all the others?

In the afternoon we took a brief excursion to Kifissia, a suburb of Athens. What beauty, what wonderful natural surroundings. We walked along the paths and running water flowed along beside us. Blessed water, I heard my father saying. It was the month of June and the world looked glorious. Birds were singing, the water was bubbling its own song, butterflies and birds were flying here and there. I quickly forgot my morning's disappointment, surrounded by so much beauty.

Time was passing by rapidly, school was more demanding now, with more work to be done. On top of that, as a daughter

From right: Erika Kounio, Rita Saltiel, Dorin Kovo, May Benrubi and Ritsa, 1939.

of 'respectable citizens' I had to learn French. Since there were no special centers for learning languages, a '*mademoiselle*' visited our house twice a week. I didn't care at all about French, and only with great difficulty did I try to master this awkward language. I had the same lack of enthusiasm for my piano lessons. My teacher, Mrs Mitza Abravanel, although my mother's close friend, never let me have any privileges, and she made me practice scales and exercises by Carl Czerny (1791–1857) for hours on end. I definitely felt very resentful at having to sit in front of the piano while my friends played outside.

I was possessed by a great question and a great disappointment ... I wanted to become a member of the youth organization (Neolea) that all my friends belonged to. But Jews were not welcome in the Metaxas youth organization. It was the first time I realized that I was not on equal terms with my Christian friends.

My disillusionment grew more when my friend Rosa's eldest sister was not permitted to join the tennis club, because they did not accept Jewish members! She wanted to become a member but was rejected.

It was 1939. A new year. Our parents were even more subdued, and my mother prepared the guest room for grandpa and grandma. The Germans had overrun the Sudetenland and there was no place for Jews there anymore. Those who could flee did so.

Grandfather and Grandmother, a suitcase in each hand, left their house and all their belongings and came to us as refugees to find shelter in their daughter's house. My brother and I were overwhelmed with joy, but they didn't share our feelings.

The clouds over Europe were thickening more and more, and in Germany people's admiration for the man who was called a 'buffoon', for Adolf Hitler, was growing stronger and stronger. The German people cheered him louder and louder.

At home, we children enjoyed our grandparents' stay so much, although we were not able to make them share our happiness. They hardly left the radio, and all the adults listened to the news together.

I can still hear Hitler's screams broadcast over the radio, the cries of '*Sieg Heil*' and the German people's standing ovations. But children as we were, we managed to enjoy our daily lessons and play periods.

2 • *German Occupation and Deportation*

On the first day of September 1939, Germany invaded Poland. That was it! The Second World War had begun.

The grown-ups around us were becoming more and more anxious with each passing day. Everyone's life now centered around the war. But what about us children? We still went to school, we played and we planned, blessed with the carefree nature of children.

For me the biggest event was that I changed schools. Now I was a student at S'china's Girls' School. I was a freshman in high school. Everything became more serious. New teachers, new friends: Maria Stangou, Ilectra, Nina Saltiel, Dorin Kovo, May Benrubi, Rita Saltiel and Roula Tari were my best friends. How much fun it was to make new friends!

Our headmistress, Mrs S'china, was a small lady, always elegantly dressed, who rarely smiled at us. As soon as we caught sight of her we stopped giggling and started to behave appropriately for her 'Girls' School'. Although she was very strict, I remember that we loved her dearly. We were also very fond of Mrs Victoria, the school caretaker, despite the fact that she picked on us. Of all our teachers, the best ones were our maths teacher, Mr Charalambakis; our physics teacher, Mr Baltas; Mrs Evnouchidou, who taught Classical Greek and Mr Michailidis. These people had a special place in my heart, and because I was so fond of them and respected them so much, I learned a lot that I still remember.

Our French teacher was also very nice, but we gave him a hard time. We would cover his chair with chalk from the blackboard erasers. Because he always wore dark trousers, the white dust stood out beautifully on his back when he stood up; sometimes we threw roasted chick-peas on the floor so that he would step on them.

Our house was full of newspapers, both Greek and foreign ones. Every evening my parents would listen to the news and follow the rapid development of events. War was not funny, but for us it was so far away.

Despite the 'hard times' everyone was predicting, 1939 came to an end and the new year began. 'Happy New Year!' we wished each other. But we looked forward to the new year, 1940, with great concern.

In 1940 the Germans were on the march. They conquered one country after another: France, Belgium, Holland, but for me the most devastating thing was my grandmother's illness. May she be well again soon, I prayed.

The first months of the year went by quickly. Spring came, joyful Easter time, then the month of June and the end of the school year. This summer we would not travel anywhere. Staying home was just fine, there was too much worry to think about travel. As usual, we children enjoyed ourselves and planned our futures. Our future studies were a topic that occupied us all. 'I will become a doctor,' I said; 'I will become an engineer like my grandfather,' answered my brother.

15 August 1940: The Greek battleship *Elli* was sunk. We all hovered around the wireless to listen to the news …

Big headlines on the front page – They sank the *Elli*! Who? The Italians … Why? Everybody was talking about it. What a provocation!

Life went on. My parents, subdued, listened to the news and followed the course of events with increasing anxiety.

28 October 1940: Metaxas' big NO to the Italians. Army mobilization. War …

I couldn't describe my excitement. Now we would show the 'macaroni-eaters' what Greece was all about.

We children also wanted to offer our services. What could we do? We were just a bunch of friends, most of us *Diaplasis* subscribers. We had formed our own club – 'The Thessalonikians' we called it. The members were Nikos Chardalias, Chrisanthos Chrisanthou, Roula Tari, Andreas Valtadoros, Nikos Sofianos, Avra Papaioannou, Kostas Labrianidis, Giorgos Nikolaidis and others. The only thing for us girls to do was to knit for the war effort. We frantically knitted gloves, socks and hoods for the soldiers. We knitted and sang Sofia Vembo's latest hit, 'Fie on you Mousolini, none of you will be left.'

Our ears were pricked up so we wouldn't miss any news. Our army was advancing and winning – who could expect anything else?

We had no idea, we children, what war was all about. It seemed like a big game. The newspapers announced one victory after another in big headlines. I remember that I went to the neighborhood news kiosk to read the headlines of the newspapers we didn't subscribe to, and I read about the victories of our army: Korytsa, Tepeleni, Argirokastro, Chimara, Agii Saranta.

Our correspondence with *Diaplasis* subscribers throughout Greece continued. We wrote about our impressions and shared our pride in our victorious army.

In addition to our anxieties about the war, we worried about my grandmother's illness.

In the theater a series of variety shows succeeded in a big way. They satirized the Italians wearing plumes on their helmets. Sofia Vembo sang various songs to inspire the army and civilian population. The newspapers kept printing big headlines about our army's victories.

Winter came earlier that year. Frost and snow in the mountains.

'Keep on knitting girls, waste no time, our soldiers are cold!'

The first few weeks went by and then the first casualties arrived. Feet with gangrene, amputated legs. The first dead, and then more and more … All the terrors of war. The cold was getting more severe. Our hearts were beginning to grow cold, and so were the songs on our lips.

I was now in the second year of high school. Together with our lessons, we had more grown-up dreams. Naturally we never stopped joking and making mischief. The things we thought of … This year seemed to have gone by faster than the others.

A tragic event in our family and a great sadness overtook me. On 26 December 1940, my darling, my most beloved grandmother, Theresa, passed away. It was my first experience of death. Why did people die? I could not cope with it.

Today, 50 years later, I realize how lucky she was to die in her bed, surrounded by her children.

The year 1941 began, more gloomy than any previous year. Besides our lessons, we followed the developments and all the news stories. Our conversations were now mostly centered around the war. Our army was resisting, despite the terrible cold weather, despite the casualties and the deaths. The Italians were surrendering and we were gaining ground … But our greatest threat was from the north. Gradually the Germans were conquering all of Europe. The big dark cloud grew bigger and spread threateningly. They were already very close; they had conquered Yugoslavia. They were close to our border. Fortunately we had the 'Metaxas line'; that would stop them.

We didn't sing with the same enthusiasm anymore. The newspapers stopped writing about victories. The casualties with amputated limbs were multiplying, and the number of deaths rising. Shock and horror!

In this way the first three months of 1941 went by. I could see that my parents were extremely worried, yet they didn't say much to us.

Fifty years ago children's upbringing was different. Children spent their time with other children, adults with other adults. Children didn't have a role to play in adult conversations, worries or problems.

Events were galloping. The 'Metaxas line' was overrun. The Germans had crossed our borders. The Germans were coming! Everywhere in town fires broke out. They were burning the warehouses so the Germans would not find anything. They set fire to the Alatinis warehouse, to the ammunition, to the gasoline, to the harbor. The depot's warehouses are opened; let the people help themselves so the enemy won't get anything!

Full of awe, we watched the fires from our veranda. My parents were speechless.

People emptied the warehouses and took as much food as possible. People came and went loaded with wares. Some rolled iron drums down the road, ones taken from the warehouses. They punched holes in them with pickaxes to let the oil pour out so the enemy wouldn't be able to use it. Each time the oil was poured out of the drums, the streets became impassable. An opportunity for people to collect oil as it spilled out. Every so often the noise of an explosion was heard and the general panic increased.

The suspense reached a peak, and on 9 April 1941 the Germans entered our city. The radio blared out the news, and people could hear the tanks rolling along the streets.

We locked ourselves in our house. Father did not go to work, mother did not make her morning shopping trip. Suddenly a big car carrying a large bright red flag with a swastika in the middle draped across the hood stopped in front of our house. My God, how frightful! Two Germans carrying metal badges on their chests climbed out of the car and asked for my father. Pale and scared my father appeared. Without further explanation they put him in the car and left. How awful! Where were they taking him? 'Would they kill him because he is a Jew,' I worried.

What relief we felt when we saw him return a few hours later safe and unharmed.

We bombarded him with questions: 'What did they do to you? Did they hit you? Were they nasty to you? What did they want?' None of these. The Germans came, advised by a collaborator, to take 'Kounio', the owner of the photographic equipment shop into custody. They needed film and cameras; they took them, and after getting what they wanted they let him go home.

What a relief it was for all of us. They did not even mention that he was Jewish.

This was our first experience and contact with the Germans.

The radio said that the Germans came as friends, not as conquerors. The music played on the radio changed, and Vembo and the variety revues were not heard anymore. German marches replaced them, along with orders, instructions and advisories for the civilian population. A new newspaper was published now, the *New Europe*.

Slowly and numbly life became routine again. Two of our house's rooms were requisitioned for a Gestapo officer. He was polite and did not harm us, although we were Jews. 'You see,' said our grandfather, who had recently arrived from Czechoslovakia, 'it is unnatural for Germans to behave badly. They are civilized, they are cultured. A nation that gave us Beethoven, Goethe and Heine could not be savage. It is only the SS who act brutally, and they are only a handful of people.'

Father went back to work as usual and we started school again. Of course our school was taken over by the Germans and we were sent to another school, Kalamari. But life seemed to return to a normal routine again.

Our parents were always on guard, always waiting for something to happen. But the Jewish population lived undisturbed, resuming its daily routine. The German officer and his orderly who lived in our house didn't bother us at all, and we all went on with our own lives. The city's landscape changed, however; German cars were everywhere on the streets and wherever you looked you saw German soldiers and SS troops.

We went to school as usual, but nothing was usual. We didn't laugh anymore as we used to, and we were all tight-lipped, especially our teachers. During break we formed little groups to exchange news.

My father received a letter from a colleague in Germany. For many years they had exchanged letters on very friendly terms. Of course the German friend knew that we were Jewish. He announced that his son Helmut was a soldier and that he was being transferred to Thessaloniki. He asked my father to accept him into his house and to help him as much as he could. As if this were the most natural thing in the world. He wrote to his colleague and friend, despite the fact that he was a Jew, and asked him to look after his son. For my parents too it was the obvious thing to do, to give a home to a friend's son.

Sure enough, after a few days Helmut Held appeared, and my father invited him to come and dine with us. After that he came to our house often and did not want to leave us. He felt that we were like his own family. He played with us children and talked with our mother.

Fifty years later I wondered if his father had known of the Nuremberg laws? Was he unaware of how much the Jews were being persecuted; did he not know that they sent them to concentration camps; had he not heard of 'Kristallnacht' – 'crystal night'? Had he not heard the anti-Semitic speeches full of hatred and virulence against the Jews? How did he dare to send his son to find a family atmosphere in the house of a Jew? Was he not afraid of censorship when he wrote letters full of gratitude for the hospitality his Jewish friend was showing his son?

The weeks went by fast. Summer came, and things became more difficult. There was a food shortage. People were trying to get supplies for the winter. One day mother found onions in the market and bought several kilos because we had found them … the same happened with potatoes, salt, sugar. Who knew what might happen? Bad news reached our ears, they had taken several hostages in reprisal for a case of sabotage and the murder of a German.

In the summer everything seemed better and easier. The

sun shone in the blue sky and the sea was so tempting. My parents worried, they had sleepless nights, constantly listening to the radio – and we … we kept on playing.

'Thank goodness we have our vineyard in Ambeli,' said my father. This was what we called a plot of land we owned in Panorama (12 kilometers from Thessaloniki), which in those days was called Arsakli. It was my father's great love. He bought the plot in 1937 or 1938, because he had always dreamed of farming. It was located in Kapoutsida, where they cultivated special grapes used to make delicious wine. That is why when we talked about our plot we called it Ambeli, which means vineyard. In those days it took a big excursion to reach Ambeli. There was no public transportation except for a few buses that went back and forth during the day. They departed from the Café Petinos in Aristotelous Square.

In 1939 my father built a small dwelling there following my grandfather's plans and under his supervision. It was our pride and joy. There was no electricity, we used a paraffin stove for cooking and 'Lux' brand paraffin lamps for light. Everything was very simple, but this little house gave us immense pleasure. We used to go every Sunday morning, carrying our food with us, and returned on foot in the evening. The road was deserted, sometimes not even a bus could be seen during our walk home. There were no houses around us, not a person in sight.

During the summer, my father decided to plant some potatoes for the bad days ahead. Giorgos Zourelidis, a local man, helped him. They will be good for both our families, he said. Father and Giorgos made plans and planted as many seeds as possible.

In those days there was very little water in Arsakli; one couldn't do everything.

My brother and I ran around catching tortoises, chasing some of the numerous rabbits and lifting stones to find snake eggs, which were also abundant in those days.

We often received visits from friends on Sundays. We

played explorers, discovering the neighboring area. Arsakli was our little paradise. For my father it was our salvation, for in the countryside everything seemed so far away.

There was very little food now. At home we counted the portions, and mother spared on oil and sugar. There was a substitute for sugar: karob syrup (made from the pods of a plant common in the Mediterranean area). Ummm! It was not bad; it was quite tasty. Fortunately there was some oil that we could spread on bread to make it tastier. Sometimes a little sugar sprinkled on top made it even better. My father worried about the potatoes: would they germinate? Would they grow?

Little by little our nation was threatened by famine. With the premature cold weather our houses froze and our hunger grew. Winter and frost intensified, and every day more and more starved and frozen people were found in the streets. Corpses were picked up every morning. What horror! What anxiety!

I caught fragments of my parents' conversation: 'You see, they leave the Jews undisturbed. Fortunately the Nuremberg law does not apply here.' They seemed to be more relieved.

Bread was rationed and they gave us yellow cornbread that looked like cake, but the taste …

Our minds turned constantly to food, and my mother concocted the most exotic dishes to feed us. I remember one time when she cooked lentils and maggots floated to the top in the boiling froth. Patiently she spooned them out until there were none left. It didn't occur to her to throw the lentils away. 'Come on,' she said, 'don't be like that, you'll see how tasty it is.'

Winter, this terrible freezing cold winter, continued. Traffic ground to a halt. We accompanied our father to his shop on foot. He was afraid to walk alone because he might slip on the icy ground. After breaking one of his legs twice in succession, it was shorter than the other, and he walked with a limp.

We went to school as usual. Some of our classmates didn't come anymore. We were told that they had left Thessaloniki.

My dearest friend, Ritza Mamouna, left in 1940. They now lived in Athens, but we corresponded frequently and exchanged news.

Our meetings with *Diaplasis* members were always regular. Our club, the Thessalonikians, was mentioned more and more on the last two pages of the classified section. Also our correspondence with other *Diaplasis* readers continued uninterrupted.

At one of our meetings our president, Roula Tari, suggested arranging a lecture. It would be a cultural contribution to our city. Why not talk about Thessalonikian composers: how about Emile Riadi?

We all liked the idea. I was extremely excited. Together with Roula and some other members we went to work. We prepared for the event while participating in other club activities. We were planning to present it the following September. We had no difficulty in finding a location. The Valayianni School agreed to let us use the biggest hall of their building. With all these preparations the winter of 1941 passed by.

Then it was 1942. Finally spring had arrived. A whole year had gone by under the German occupation, and we could definitely feel its presence. Meanwhile the German borders spread. There was a war going on in Africa, and another in Russia.

We heard that they were taking more and more hostages. The resistance was also growing, and every so often we heard of sabotage by the partisans. Our conversations became more serious and our lessons more 'informal'. The Thessalonikians continued to meet regularly, and Roula was preparing her lecture on Emile Riadi. We discussed the details and prepared ourselves.

Then suddenly there was a great upheaval in the midst of the apparent calm of the Jewish community. A German decree called for all Jews aged eighteen to forty-five to gather in

Erika Kounio, 28 August 1942.

Elevtherias Square at 8.00 a.m. on 11 July 1942. What we had feared was happening, the last card was being dealt.

Why did they want them? What would they do to them? What would they do to us? These were the adults' questions, and we listened and listened, unable to utter a word …

At home you only heard this sort of conversation: 'They took them all and sent them to serve as forced laborers.

They need them for TODT (a paramilitary engineering organization whose founder's name was Todt). How long would they keep them? Would they suffer? And the name 'Merten' was mentioned increasingly at home.

And we, like all children, continued to play and swim. We were all together, Christian children, Jewish children, all wonderful friends.

I heard my father talking about negotiations between Merten and the Jewish Community. I didn't understand much and, as usual, my parents whispered in private, never in front of us. We could only barely catch bits of their conversations …

Then suddenly another bomb exploded, this time in our family. Three German police cars stopped in front of our house. Wild-looking Germans entered our home. They searched it.

I ran to my room to hide, or better to get rid of a little brooch that I had with two flags on it, one English and one Greek. In my innocence I threw it out the window to one of my friends standing below. The Germans searched the house. When they finished they called mother, father and grandfather to get ready to follow them.

I heard the Germans talking among themselves, deciding whether they should take us, the children, as well. They asked my father our ages and to my surprise I heard him taking some years off our actual ages. 'They are young, let them stay here,' I heard one of them saying, and they left. What a fright! What happened? Where were they taking them?

My brother and I, bewildered, watched them get into one of the cars together with our grandfather and drive off. We were left on our own not knowing what was happening. I must do something, I am the oldest, I must protect my little brother! I notified one of our shop's employees, my father's brother, some friends, and then we waited. Only the next day did we find out that they had put them in the Gestapo prison in an old house located at Vasilissis Olga Street 31. Friends of my parents arrived and tried to find out what had happened. One thing was for sure, they told us, they didn't imprison them on account of their being Jewish. There must have been a different reason.

My brother and I were now living at home on our own. During the day a woman came to look after us – a dear old cleaning lady – and she left in the afternoon. Two or three days later my father managed to send us a message about what we should do and instructing us to give a camera to the messenger as he had promised. The messenger was a German soldier, I don't remember anymore if he was an SS-man.

He was one of the prison guards to whom my father had promised a camera as a present. He was scared and took every precaution. It was late, after 10.00p.m., when the bell rang. We were on our own at home, and without thinking twice I went down to open the door. The man was extremely polite, gave us the message, and I gave him the camera. He was impressed that I spoke German so fluently. After that he came back twice, bringing news and instructions from father. Father asked us to bring mother's medication to the prison. How could we bring it there, it was impossible, unrealistic, our people said!

Again, in my childish innocence, I considered going to the Gestapo, talking to them, pleading with them. I knew an officer who was a friend of the officer who stayed in our house. ('Our officer' was away on leave. He had sent somebody to pick up his things, and we never saw him again. They never replaced him in our requisitioned room.) I had learned from him where their offices were – somewhere on Aristotelous Square, and I set off.

I trembled from head to foot, and I remember that I pinched my cheeks so I wouldn't appear too pale. I looked the guard straight in the eye and in German asked him for permission to meet Officer So-and-So – and in fact he brought me to his office!

I remember vividly how I was approached by two or three uniformed men who asked me what I was doing there, what

I wanted. They were very impressed that I spoke German so fluently. I said that I had come to obtain permission to bring my mother's medicine to the place where she was being held. She was very ill and required a strict diet.

I still don't know how I managed. The fact is that they gave me a piece of paper authorizing me to bring her the special nourishment and medication she needed every day. With the paper clutched in my hand I left. Up until then there had been no measures against the Jews. The army was still an army of occupation. For a whole month, as long as my parents were at the Gestapo prison, I went there every day at noon. I knocked on the iron door, a little window would open, I would show the authorization paper, and they accepted the pot containing my mother's food.

Meanwhile, friends and acquaintances did their best to arrange their release. We were constantly afraid, because every so often we would hear that they had taken hostages from the prison and shot them in reprisal.

Late in the evenings friends would come over to keep us company and to discuss the details of our arrangements for the Riadis lecture. Despite our anxiety, we were still just children, with youth's nonchalance; we laughed and we enjoyed listening to our friend Christanthos (Soulis) Christanthou playing his favorite pieces on the piano.

My father's friends did everything possible to get our parents out of the Gestapo prison. A month later we heard the good news: they had moved them to the Eptaphyrgion prison.

It was a whole different world there. We could go and visit them; the prison director was an old acquaintance of my father. They let us know that they needed blankets and clothing. How could we carry all the things? There was no transportation to Eptaphyrgion. So our friends got together with us and we found a solution. Soultana's son (Soultana was the housekeeper who was looking after us) had a cart, the kind traveling tradesmen used to put their goods in and pull them around the streets. Fantastic! We would load the cart and all of us would push it from Luxembourg, where our house was located, all the way to Eptaphyrgion. Unfortunately, my brother couldn't come with us, because he had stepped on a nail and his foot was in a bad state. So there was one less person to push. After many hours we arrived at the prison and I was permitted to visit my parents for five minutes. They gave me instructions about whom to contact, which lawyer to address to continue the proceedings for obtaining their release.

Things were looking up, and my parents' friends reassured us that they would soon be freed. Every other day I went to visit them for a while. I got used to the long walk. My brother was still unable to come, and quite often I was accompanied by one of my friends.

The day for the Riadi lecture was approaching. We prepared the invitations and everything else that was needed. My parents were still in prison, but I had their permission and blessing to attend the lecture.

It was Sunday morning, a sunny September day. The attendance was big, many of the city's leading personalities came, including the mayor. It was a very successful event. We were all so happy, so pleased that we had managed it successfully. We received congratulations, and our faces beamed with happiness and pride. Our only disappointment was that our parents were not with us. Two days later they let them go free.

'What happened, why did they put you in prison,' we asked father. The reason was Helmut, our German friend's son who had visited our home. He had not stayed in Thessaloniki for very long before being transferred to the island of Crete. He sent a letter to my parents thanking them for their hospitality. He went on to say in his letter that many preparations were being made for the war in Africa. I don't know exactly what he wrote, but this was my father's answer to our questions. It seems that he was in an anti-Nazi movement there and was being closely watched. As my father heard later, Helmut got drunk one night and cursed Hitler in the most explicit way. The censors had stopped his letters to my parents and imprisoned them in an effort to find out more about Helmut. With all the initiatives our friends and lawyers took, they managed to prove that our parents were innocent and so they were set free. Fifty years later I wonder whether one reason they let them go free was because they knew that they would soon arrest them again.

As far as Helmut was concerned, we learned that the National Socialists had imprisoned and condemned him to death. Although we were together again, reunited, life was not the same as before, even though we all returned to our old routines. We heard that many Jews had left to join the partisans in the mountain. There was a lot of talk about sabotage and explosions, etc.

On 1 October 1942 school started again as usual. I was now in my third year of high school. Like all children, we were looking forward to meeting our old classmates, but sad that the holidays were over.

The atmosphere at school was different. We were not carefree anymore. The occupation had changed us all. From my Jewish classmates I heard about the men who had been taken away to do forced labor. They took Rosa's uncle, and sent him back a very sick man. He was a shadow of his former self, Rosa said, and he couldn't seem to pull himself together again. They had been forced to work under the burning sun, Rosa said. They had not given them enough to eat, and many had collapsed from exhaustion.

Rita's cousin was taken, as was Dorin's. They took Sarika's father, and she cried constantly. During our break we formed little circles, and each of us had something to say that she had heard at home: about the resistance that was getting stronger, and the sabotage and about somebody who had left for the mountains – but be careful not to talk about these things to anybody. Everything was very confusing.

Our grandfather tried to learn Greek and be a good friend to us and our friends. I remember one time when we wanted to go on an excursion, boys and girls together, to Oreokastro for a whole day! Boys and girls couldn't possibly go without a chaperon; my father was unyielding. Even if my brother went with us. After a lot of persuasion and whining father said: 'OK you can go, but grandfather must go with you'. 'Grandfather!' I said, thunderstruck. 'What will our friends say? They will tease me!' Still, my longing to go on this excursion was so great that I broke the news to my friends. My friends knew grandfather and were very fond of him. They didn't object at all.

I think the other girls' parents were also relieved to know that there would be a grown-up with us. It was one of the best excursions I ever went on. My grandfather, with his big mustache and bald head – who seemed very old to me! – proved to be our best pal. He improvised interesting games; he played ball with us. And we all said with one voice: 'Grandfather should come with us on all our excursions.' How proud I felt of my grandfather!

It must have been November, still 1942, when one evening – as we did every evening – we were listening to the BBC news on the wireless. All the windows were tightly closed and the front door double-locked. At a certain point the news announcer said, in a very casual tone, that the same morning two Polish Jews had arrived at the radio station. They had escaped from a camp named Lublin. There – the announcer went on in the same indifferent voice – mass murders of Jews were going on.

Without any additional comment he continued reporting the news.

I will never forget my grandfather's face. He stood up, red in the face, with big angry eyes and switched the radio off. He then turned to my parents and said: 'Rubbish, that is English propaganda.' He himself had come to Greece three years earlier from Czechoslovakia, a persecuted refugee, to find shelter at his daughter's home in Greece, yet he still believed the Germans were a superior race! And all that London was reporting was propaganda!

Meanwhile, it must have been around mid-October, we heard that all the men compelled to do forced labor had returned. They were ill, thin, wretched. Many had died. I cannot remember many details, only my parents' relief.

Soon after that there was another scare for the Jews.

Mother, father and grandfather were all very upset. It could not be possible – but indeed, they were destroying the Jewish Cemetery. My friend May Benrubi came to school one day crying. They had turned her father's shop into an army center. Sarika bid us farewell, because they were leaving for Athens to stay with her grandmother. We were all thoroughly upset. We could not concentrate on our lessons, instead we all gathered in small circles discussing what we had heard at home.

In this way the weeks went by during a very cold winter. It was the second year of occupation, and a new year was starting without much hope.

Who knew what would be in store for us in 1943?

The hardships of the occupation were enormous; there was less and less food; people were dying from cold and hunger. There were more cold and hungry people huddled on the sidewalks; many had already died. I heard talk about the black market and about the difficulties of finding food. After the Christmas break we started school again.

Father went to work every day, and every day he came back gloomier, bringing bad news. Something had to be done, and the only thing I knew was that he was transferring the title to his shop to a photographer friend of his from Serres, so that it wouldn't be expropriated by the German army. From then on his shop was not registered under his name.

January slipped by and then it was February. It was very cold and the streets were frozen. It was Saturday when father came home from the shop bringing us some very bad news. 'A special SS committee came, led by two men named Brunner and Wisliceny,' I heard him say to mother. 'I don't like the looks of things.'

And indeed, things were really not at all good.

On 8 February, at noon on Monday, news began to circulate in the Jewish community. Black despair gripped the Jewish population, for the Germans had decided to impose the Nuremberg laws in Thessaloniki. Family and friends gathered at our house. They were in despair, they talked about the SS orders. All the Jews were now required to put a yellow star on every piece of clothing they wore. Jews were not allowed to use public transportation. All the Jews had to move to special areas the SS had specified, i.e., ghettos. Did that mean we had to leave our home? Go to another place to live?

My father hurried out to find housing in the area where Jews were permitted to live. Mother tried to calm us. 'Oh, well! It is not so terrible, we will all wear a yellow star, so what? This way they will recognize the Jews! Don't worry, father is looking for a house, in a few days we shall move.'

The very next day we started wearing our yellow stars, but we went to school as usual. I still remember the love and tenderness our teachers and our classmates showed us. Nothing had changed, I thought, and our lives would go on, wearing the yellow stars.

But we were very tense, though we tried to behave normally.

At lunch father always had something new to tell us. He did not go to his shop any more, but he visited the Jewish community offices every day. It took him a week to find a little house where we could move, fortunately within the boundaries set by the SS. It was so tiny that grandpa couldn't stay with us.

So, we moved to our new residence two weeks later, and grandfather went to live as the guest of a Christian Bulgarian family, very close to our house.

We took only a few pieces of furniture with us, the most essential. We gave our piano and our rugs to one of our neighbors, who promised to look after them until we returned. Our sitting room furniture, together with the carved wooden bookcase full of my father's and mother's books, our hand-carved desk and our beautiful oak dining room set were placed in the care of a photographer named Melanidis, a very good friend of my father. My mother's and grandmother's jewelry was entrusted to another good friend. Mr Melanidis later returned everything we had entrusted to him in perfect condition. The rest of the things were sold to help people survive the hardships of the occupation.

We loaded our things into carts and set off pushing them towards our new residence. The roads were full of big wagons, little wagons, bicycles loaded with mattresses, beds, chairs, suitcases and bundles. Men were pushing, children young and old helped as best they could, and women were following, babies in their arms or dragging their children by the hand.

People filled with despair were pouring into the streets and alleys. I heard their voices. 'Come on, push a bit harder, Moschiko, Maki, Rachel don't wander off!' There was a steady hum of voices. The whole world looked dark under the black cloud bearing down upon us. Living in the little house in Miaouli Street, we were still permitted to attend school, much to our own satisfaction. This made our days richer. We could still chat with our classmates, but we did not laugh at all anymore. We were very serious and very worried.

After school I did not go straight home. I had to visit first our old house at Koromila Street; I couldn't bear to be separated from it. It was so empty and quiet. I went through the yard to the platform. I stood there filled with sadness watching the sea, the White Tower. I waited till sunset bathed the sky in shades of pink, and I counted the many distant windows illuminated by the orange of the setting sun. It was then that I spoke to God, praying with all my soul's strength for our suffering to end.

My walks from school to our old house and then to Miaouli Street did not continue for long. We had hardly stayed for a week in our new house when a new SS order forbade us to be outside the ghetto after sunset. Now I had to return from school very quickly, to be there before sunset.

One day I was so overcome by nostalgia that I took off my

star and without saying anything went one last time to see our house in Koromila Street. I sat by the sea to bid farewell to the sun. It was to be the last time for many years. Mother and father were waiting for me at home, very worried and upset. I promised them not to do this again. A few days later the Jews were forbidden to leave the ghetto even in the daytime.

How thrilled I felt when my Christian friends came to visit us in the ghetto. It was so kind, so moving, and all our friends came to see us. Some of them came every day!

In the ghetto, which was full of people aimlessly wandering about in the streets or gathering in small groups, everybody was weighed down by a great sense of despair.

Every day there were new orders. To confiscate all the Jew's assets. To put a yellow star on every shop, house, office.

One day I heard them talking about deportation: 'They will take us all to a different place.' 'Does that mean exile?' I asked father.

That very day our old neighborhood postman came to see father in our house. I heard him saying to my parents, 'Give me the two children and I will take them to my mother, to the village, just outside Veria. They will be fine there – you must not worry.'

And my father's answer, 'No, thank you. Thank you very much, but I don't want my family to be split up.' The next few days we spoke more and more about deportation. 'They will take us all,' the know-it-alls were saying, 'to Cracow, a Polish city. We shall live and work there together.' Grandfather came to eat with us every day. We children loved talking to him. I remember him telling us: 'You shouldn't worry or be afraid. Naturally we shall have to work where they take us, and food will not be as tasty as your mother's. We shall have to wear dark underwear and dark shirts.' Of all possibilities, these were the most terrible things that could happen to us, as far as our incorrigible grandfather was concerned. He still believed in the superiority of the German race.

It was 10 March 1943 when, early in the morning, an SS car

stopped in front of our house. They ordered father to collect our most necessary clothes and said we must leave in the next two hours – or about that soon, if I remember rightly – to go to Baron Hirsch, a part of town near the railway station. How? What with? Where shall we put our suitcases?

'That is your problem,' answered the SS-men.

Fortunately, grandfather was not at home, and father sent somebody to warn him to stay where he was and hide.

I don't know where or how we found a cart and loaded it with our suitcases and some food. But this is how our little caravan set off to cross the town on foot. We arrived at the Baron Hirsch ghetto in two or three hours.

We pushed the cart with our heads lowered, each lost in his own dark musings. It must have been terrible for my parents. For my brother and me it was like an unhappy part of a great adventure. When you are young, adult terror and despair does not touch you in the same way.

When we arrived at the Baron Hirsch ghetto, we were immediately surrounded by the Jewish community's clerks, who bombarded my parents with questions: 'Why did you come alone? Why did they send you here? Why? Why?'

My father learned the reason later from a militiaman. One of the informers, either Boudourian or Papanahum – I heard both these names – had betrayed us to the SS. He had told them that father had given his shop to a Christian in order to save his assets. The SS's immediate reaction was to apprehend us and send us to the Baron Hirsch ghetto.

I remember the impression the place made on me. It was jammed with people. Men, women, children, babies in perpetual aimless motion. They did not know where to put us. 'We don't have any space, nothing, really nothing ...,' I heard one of the community representatives say to my father. It was raining and freezing cold. Finally we went to an old café with broken windows. The roof leaked, and there were puddles of water on the cement floor.

Mother, who was always so strong and so clever at finding

solutions, was in desperation, and father put our things in a corner that looked a bit more sheltered.

Our living conditions were terrible. We were cold and hungry, and because of our cold and despair we couldn't sleep that night.

The next day father went to the community's 'offices' to try to find better quarters, but it was impossible, as he explained to us. They had so many people that the available housing was already overcrowded.

Another terrible night followed, with the rain dripping from the roof into little tin containers we had arranged to catch the drips. Emptying them as soon as they were full, shivering in the cold, we began another day.

Father went back to the 'offices' to find out what was happening. He came back very upset after a while to tell us that the 'deportation' was beginning. That they would take us to Poland and we could even change Greek drachmas for Polish zlotys, so we wouldn't arrive there without money.

The German trap was well prepared, and their great deceit very well studied.

With a sense of great anxiety and misery our second day in the Baron Hirsch ghetto came to an end. The next day everyone was talking about the railroad cars at the train station. Michael Molho writes in his book *In Memoriam* that there were 40 railway wagons. Forty wagons! An endless line, and they were waiting to be loaded.

Eventually father came in a rush to speak to mother – not to us – to ask her what she thought about our leaving with the first transport.

One of the community clerks suggested taking him off the list so we could leave later. One never knows what will happen. But our fate had already been decided! Mother, discouraged by the terrible living conditions, said to him, stressing every word: 'Salvator, whatever will be, let it happen as soon as possible. Let's leave at the first opportunity.'

That was it, we would leave with everybody else in the first transport. The cards were on the table, without much discussion or hesitation.

And in the midst of our misfortune, this was our luck, to be in the first transport.

I have often wondered what it was that made possible the survival of my whole family – father, mother, my brother and myself? Luck, destiny, coincidence? Maybe all three together, and one of the coincidences was that we found ourselves in the first transport.

Fifty years later, I cannot believe how everything happened! How were the Germans able to trick and mislead so many people? They prepared their plans so systematically and cleverly and slowly set their trap, so that in a single month – after they revealed their true selves – they managed to assemble so many people and convince them that nothing terrible was happening.

In my mind all their orders about the yellow star, the confiscation of property, the prohibitions, first not to circulate on the main roads, then not to leave the ghetto at all – all those orders seemed to have been given over a period of months. It seemed as though after each order several weeks passed before a new one was given.

I remember saying, and hearing other people say: 'So, we shall have to wear a star; it is not so terrible.' And then: 'So, we will have to declare our assets, let this be the worse and nothing else.' 'So, we have to move to a smaller house and live with all the Jews together; it doesn't matter. It will be good to have all the families together.' But the orders came one after another, without giving us time to figure out what was happening.

When – in 1976 – I read Michael Molho's book *Thirty Years after the Persecution* for the first time, I could hardly believe that the measures against the Jews began to be imposed on 8 February 1943, and by 25 February 1943 the whole Jewish population had been moved to the ghettos. And 17 days later the first transport departed, with 2,800 panic-stricken people crammed into 35 railway wagons – destination Poland.

Unbelievable, unimaginable! And ever since I read this, each time I recall what happened, I experience the same awful feeling of wonder and exasperation, that it could not have been possible.

And 50 years later when I decided to write my own memories, I referred to many books in order to verify that these dates were correct. Looking back now, 50 years later, I believe it would not have been possible for the Jews to have reacted any differently.

The orders fell like the blows of a whip, one after the other. Confused, overwhelmed, terrified the Jews succumbed to their fate. 'After all, they will be together again, wherever they are brought.' Hadn't the rabbi confirmed that they would all be reunited in Cracow? Hadn't they changed all their money to Polish zlotys? 'Let's not make things worse than they are. The main thing is to keep our families together!' Optimism and hope always had the upper hand. 'We are going through a bad time, but it will end!'

Some, courageous and perceptive persons without families, escaped to the mountains. And some of the wealthier people managed to hide on an island or in some remote village – but there were very few who did.

Fifty years later, bending over my books and this white paper, I tried to understand once more how was it possible for such a terrible thing to happen. I have tried to understand in order to explain to my seven grandchildren, and especially to my eldest grandson – 25 years old – who I know cannot understand or excuse that so many thousands of people – nearly 50,000 – let themselves be herded like sheep to the slaughter.

How can I make him understand the times we lived in? Eighty per cent of the Jewish population spoke Spanish better than Greek. It was only in 1932 that a new law was passed that all Greek children should have compulsory education in the Greek school system for the first six grades. Parents and grandparents spoke only Spanish, so their children learned both Spanish and Greek.

How could he understand that to hide or to reach the mountains was difficult, because Jews could be recognized as non-Christians by their accents and risked being betrayed to the Germans.

And that even to hide they needed money – a lot of money which they did not have. Eighty per cent of the Jewish population were poor workers, porters, artisans or small merchants.

Yes, some of the young people managed to escape the persecution and flee to the mountains. The partisans encouraged them to join their cause; they would have helped them to escape. But how could others leave their families?

My husband was the child of a mixed marriage; his mother was a Christian. Dr Max Merten, head of the military administration of Thessaloniki, had decreed a law of protection for the families of mixed marriages. The lawyer Georgios Papailiakis was the person who worked for this decree, which saved 19 'mixed' families. The rationale was that the Jewish husband had to stay behind in order to support a Christian mother and her children! If the Christian wife were to die, he would lose this protection and would suffer the same fate as the rest of his people. This is why my future husband's family remained in Thessaloniki.

My husband, who spoke German, was employed as an interpreter in the fire brigade. In the fire brigade there was a resistance movement. One of their activities was helping people flee to the mountains, German and Italian deserters among them. Having this ability – to get people to the mountains – he urged his Jewish friends, his classmates, to flee to the mountains. He always got the same response – 'How could I leave my family?'

The strength of Jewish family ties is well known. How could we leave mother and father on their own to fend for the younger children? Families were big in those days: three to five children was not unusual.

I remember how impressed I was when I first read Marcel Natzaris' journal (*Chronicle 1939–1945*, Thessaloniki, 1991), the

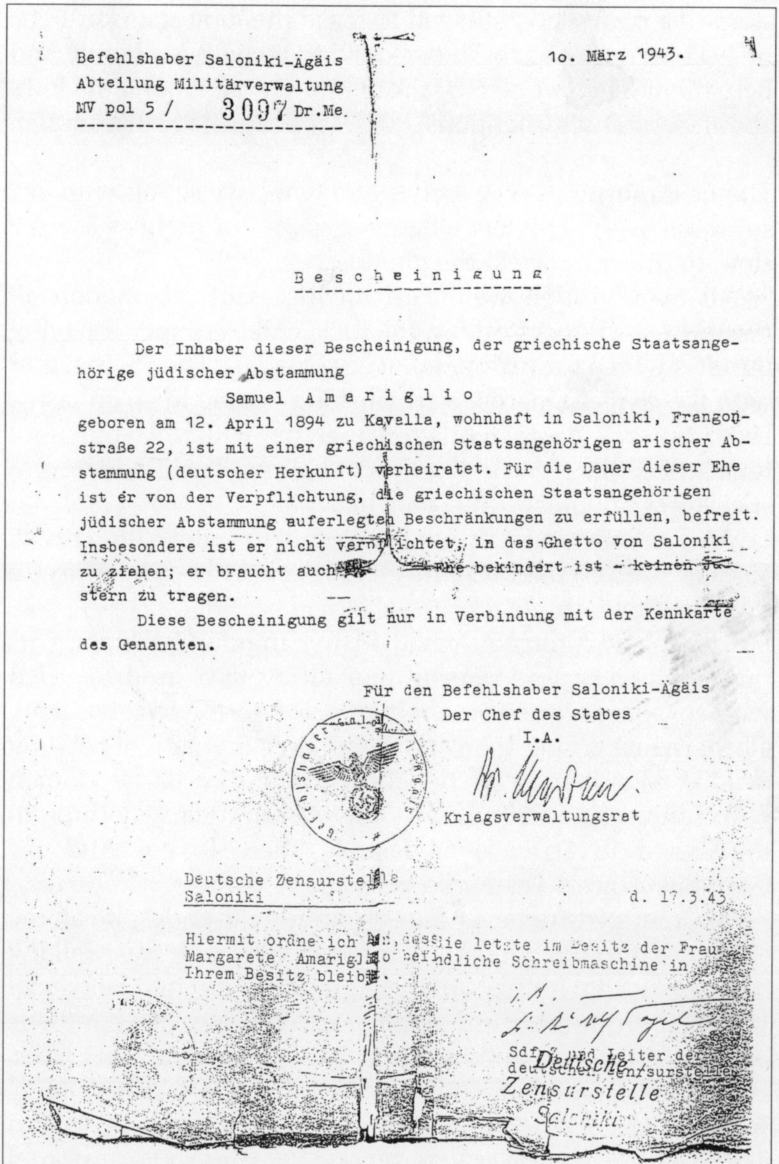

Befehlshaber Saloniki-Ägäis
Abteilung Militärverwaltung
MV pol 5 / 3097 Dr.Me.

1o. März 1943.

B e s c h e i n i g u n g

Der Inhaber dieser Bescheinigung, der griechische Staatsangehörige jüdischer Abstammung

Samuel A m a r i g l i o

geboren am 12. April 1894 zu Kavella, wohnhaft in Saloniki, Frangonstraße 22, ist mit einer griechischen Staatsangehörigen arischer Abstammung (deutscher Herkunft) verheiratet. Für die Dauer dieser Ehe ist er von der Verpflichtung, die griechischen Staatsangehörigen jüdischer Abstammung auferlegten Beschränkungen zu erfüllen, befreit. Insbesondere ist er nicht verpflichtet, in das Ghetto von Saloniki zu ziehen; er braucht auch [illegible] Ehe bekindert ist - keinen Ju- stern zu tragen.

Diese Bescheinigung gilt nur in Verbindung mit der Kennkarte des Genannten.

Für den Befehlshaber Saloniki-Ägäis
Der Chef des Stabes
I.A.
[signature]
Kriegsverwaltungsrat

Deutsche Zensurstelle
Saloniki

d. 17.3.43

Hiermit ordne ich an, dass die letzte im Besitz der Frau Margarete Amariglio befindliche Schreibmaschine in Ihrem Besitz bleibt.

i.A.
[signature]
Sdf.[illegible] und Leiter der deutschen Zensurstelle
Deutsche Zensurstelle Saloniki

Certificate granting Erika Kounio's late father-in-law, Samuel Amariglio, freedom from the restrictions normally imposed on Jewish people, as a result of his 'Aryan' marriage.

story of a man who managed to reach the mountains in 1941. In 1942 he returned to Thessaloniki to be with his family and help them. This suggests a lack of knowledge among the Jews about Germany's intentions. But let me return to 50 years ago.

The next morning, very early – at dawn – we set off with our suitcases ready. The café where we spent our nights was very close to the entrance to the ghetto.

All of a sudden we heard an incessant commotion all around us. Mothers calling for their children, men carrying bundles which they dropped every so often. The SS, together with the civilian guards, were pushing people to go on faster, faster, faster ... And I stood there together with my family, and for a little while I watched the incredible spectacle, wide-eyed, speechless, my heart thumping like crazy.

At a certain moment we too began to follow the crowd. Father talked to us constantly, telling us not to stray away, to stay close to each other.

This picture remains vivid in my mind. The four of us proceeding like one person, and all around us disheveled women, some with babies in their arms, trying to calm them, all the while crying themselves, another dragging a bawling child in each hand, elderly people trying to walk faster, men with suitcases and bundles trying to push their way through the crowd to arrive even faster! Where to go? And the Germans' voices! Their wild yells ...

Another picture never fades from my mind despite all the years. Next to me, an old grandfather, very old, was walking hand-in-hand with his wife. The grandmother had her shawl wrapped around her shoulders, and with her free hand she was clutching her walking stick. Her eyes, wide, dark eyes, stared right and left, frightened; and they were walking, walking! At a certain moment she turned her head and looked up at her husband. Her look changed, a faint smile appeared on her face and she looked up at him with such tenderness, telling him something. And then I lost sight of them as they disappeared in the crowd.

I don't know how long this march lasted. We arrived in front of the railway cars. 'Don't move from here,' father said. 'We will wait ...'

I continued to look around, unable to understand what was happening. Screams, yelling, wailing, in front of the railway car doors ... people were disappearing, disappearing into the depths of the cars, more and more ...

Hurry up! What are you waiting for? A mother reached out to help her child, and a man pushed an old man and woman who could not manage to climb up into the car by themselves. Suddenly I heard a different noise, very loud. They started to close the doors of the railway cars and attach locks ...

Germans, not SS-men, would accompany the train. Later I learned that they were policemen – *Schupos*. The head *Schupo* – I don't know how he had learned that my father spoke German – approached father and said: 'Wait, don't get in yet, I need you as an interpreter.'

This was another coincidence. My father's knowledge of German helped us to survive. Of all the people in the first group, nobody, but nobody at all, spoke German! Most were simple people, workers and artisans, porters, small merchants who spoke Spanish and many who also knew French, but no German-speakers. People were needed to act as interpreters and translate German orders.

Packed together, dragging their children and luggage, people disappeared into the railway cars. On each car a sign specified: 'Capacity 40 soldiers or eight horses.'

The cars were painted in a rusty red color, they had no windows at all apart from a skylight, very high up, left and right, protected by wire. As the doors shut you could not see anything inside; you could hardly hear anything. You saw only an occasional hand through a skylight.

Bamm! Bamm! The doors closed one after the other. We too got in. Our car was completely filled. There was no place to stretch our legs. Men, women, children and elderly people were talking, crying, complaining all at the same time. In one corner of the railway car there was a sack full of biscuits, wormy figs and olives. In the middle of the car was a pail for our 'bodily necessities'.

The four of us, crammed next to each other, sat without speaking. We just sat there with our legs folded under us – and all around us, from one side to the other, people, people … Over us was the skylight, where a bit of fresh air came in. A tall man stood up under the skylight and put his little boy on his shoulders to look outside.

After they shut the doors the train started to move. Where were we going? How long would we be shut in there? Would they give us food? My God how desperate! Some babies never stopped crying, sometimes quietly, sometimes screaming. Women were lamenting and some of the men took out their prayer books and were quietly singing hymns. It was dark in the railroad car, and they couldn't see to read, but they kept their eyes open, they turned the pages, they knew every line by heart.

Next to me sat Esterina. She had lived in Baron Hirsch; we became friends. We were the same age and shared our stories with each other.

Clickety-clack, clickety-clack, the train went on without stopping. Night fell, and the babies did not cry as much any more. Silence filled the car. Only the moans of the sick were heard. Each of us was alone, sunk in our despair and the loss of hope.

Little by little I fell asleep. The first night went by.

A new day dawned and we waited for our turn to approach the bucket and answer the call of nature. How humiliated I felt the first time. I was so embarrassed that I couldn't do anything. Fortunately a woman near by held a blanket round me to hide me from other people's eyes.

The bucket was soon full; the smell in our car was suffocating. Oh please! Some air, some fresh air, some space to stretch our legs.

The relentless clickety-clack, clickety-clack went on without stopping.

Suddenly it stopped. What had happened? What will happen? Moschiko again climbed up on his father's shoulders to peep through the skylight to see where we were.

The door opened and a Schupo called to my father to come out. My father went from one car to the next explaining what must be done. Nobody, but nobody, was allowed to get out as long as we were at the station. Only a few men would go to empty the buckets and some to fill bottles with water.

As the door opened there was a blast of fresh air and we all moved towards the opening to breathe.

There were many sick people but not a single doctor. From the car next to ours they removed a dead man – lucky him!

The first full day of our journey was over. The situation in the wagon was becoming more and more unbearable. A whole day spent in darkness. The light that filtered through the skylights was weak. It didn't reduce the darkness – and the babies cried constantly.

Thanks to my father's efforts, on the third day the head of our transport agreed to stop the train somewhere away from a station and permitted people to get out of the cars for half-an-hour. We must have been in Yugoslavia. The surroundings were deserted, not a soul to be seen. Father went from one car to the next trying to comfort people.

The *Schupos*, guns ready, watched us, and whenever someone strayed too far they ordered him back.

They did not allow us to get out of the cars again. Three more days passed in this way. The train made frequent stops, and people would try to peer out through the skylights to find out where we were. As if it would have made any difference to know exactly where we were ...

3 • *Arrival in Auschwitz and Birkenau*

It was 20 March 1943. Another stop, but this time they opened the doors. Wild cries, dogs barking, noise: '*Raus*' … '*Raus*' … '*Raus*' …

It was pitch dark and huge spotlights pierced the darkness, blinding us. '*Steigt schnell aus*!' (Climb out at once!), they were yelling: '*Schnell! Schnell!*,' (Faster! Faster!) – but nobody understood. Stunned by the long journey, stiff, hungry, frightened, desperate, everyone tried to jump out of the railroad cars, throwing their bundles and suitcases to the ground. There was confusion, screaming. The SS were running about everywhere, some with revolvers in their hands, others with whips, shouting, '*Los! … Los! … Raus! … Raus! … Schnell! … Schnell!*' (Come on! Come on! Out! Out! Faster! Faster!)

The SS-men held dogs on leashes, and the dogs barked ferociously. Baring their teeth and growling, they tried to break loose and throw themselves on us. I still remember, as though it were happening now, how I looked at them in complete astonishment. It suddenly struck me that I could not tell who were more savage, the SS-men or their dogs.

The cold was terrible, it froze our faces, hands and feet. We were chilled to the bone. Mothers held their babies tightly in their arms, and the older children clung to their skirts.

In front of the railroad cars, apart from the SS, there were men in striped clothes with shaven heads. They assisted people in climbing out of the railroad cars. They tried to tell us something, their eyes filled with horror and sympathy.

They were prisoners in the Sonderkommando (crematorium detachment), trying to assemble our baggage. How many of them met their own relatives and friends in this way … How horrifying!

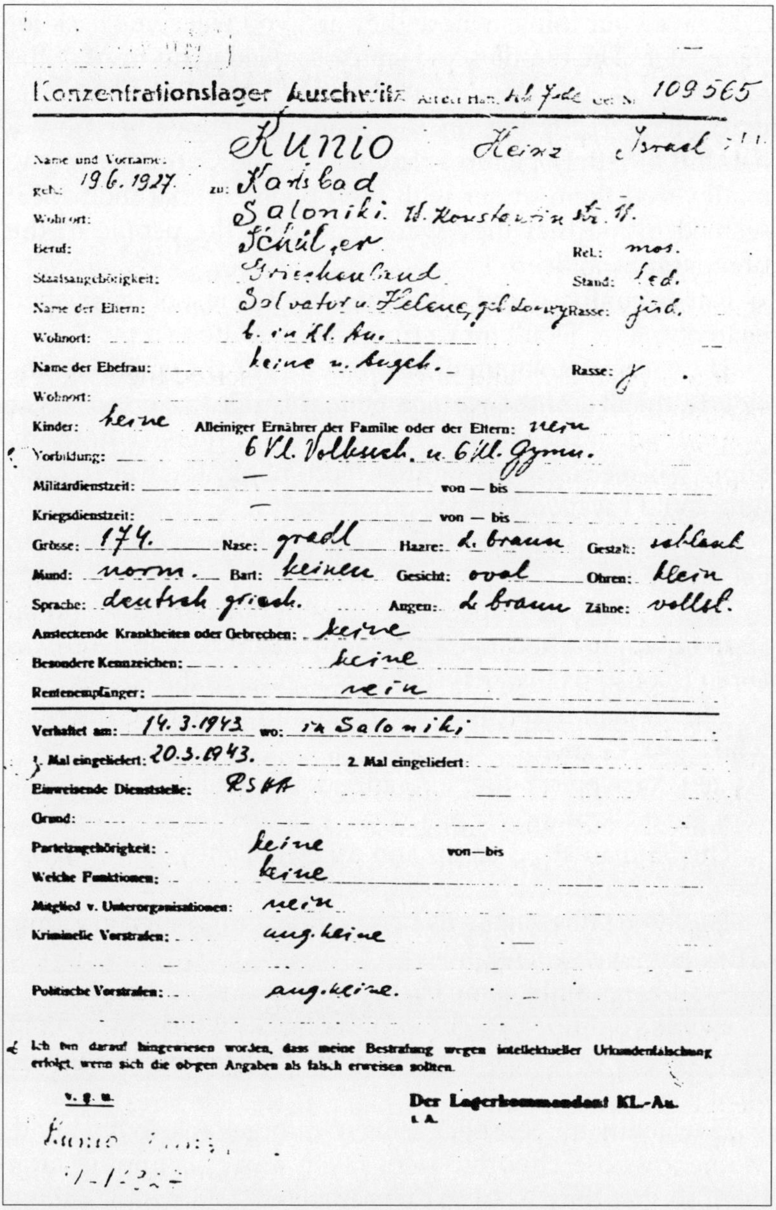

Konzentrationslager Auschwitz Art der Haft: Sch. Jude Gef. Nr. 109565

Name und Vorname: Kunio Heinz Israel

geb.: 19.6.1927 zu: Karlsbad

Wohnort: Saloniki. W. Konstantin str. 11.

Beruf: Schüler Rel.: mos.

Staatsangehörigkeit: Griechenland Stand: led.

Name der Eltern: Salvator u. Helene, geb. Lowy Rasse: jüd.

Wohnort: b. im Kl. Au.

Name der Ehefrau: keine u. Angeh. Rasse: J.

Wohnort:

Kinder: keine Alleiniger Ernährer der Familie oder der Eltern: nein

Vorbildung: 6 Kl. Volksch. u. 6 Kl. Gymn.

Militärdienstzeit: — von — bis

Kriegsdienstzeit: — von — bis

Grösse: 174. Nase: gerade Haare: d. braun Gestalt: schlank

Mund: norm. Bart: keinen Gesicht: oval Ohren: klein

Sprache: deutsch griech. Augen: d. braun Zähne: vollst.

Ansteckende Krankheiten oder Gebrechen: keine

Besondere Kennzeichen: keine

Rentenempfänger: nein

Verhaftet am: 14.3.1943 wo: in Saloniki

1. Mal eingeliefert: 20.3.1943. 2. Mal eingeliefert:

Einweisende Dienststelle: RSHA

Grund:

Parteizugehörigkeit: keine von—bis

Welche Funktionen: keine

Mitglied v. Unterorganisationen: nein

Kriminelle Vorstrafen: ang. keine

Politische Vorstrafen: ang. keine

Ich bin darauf hingewiesen worden, dass meine Bestrafung wegen intellektueller Urkundenfälschung erfolgt, wenn sich die obigen Angaben als falsch erweisen sollten.

v. g. u. Der Lagerkommandant KL.-Au.

i. A.

Kunio Heinz

Heinz Kounio's registration form at Auschwitz, 20 March 1943.

'Leave your things where they are, you will come back for them later.' The bundles and suitcases piled up in front of the railroad cars. A suitcase opened as it fell out of a railroad car, its contents scattering on the ground. I remember how a handful of family pictures flew about. The Germans, yelling loudly, trod them under with their boots. At that moment it seemed to me that they were trampling the people in the photographs to death.

Father, confused and frightened like the rest of us, pushed us to one side. 'Don't move from the spot,' he told us.

The Germans shouted out orders: 'All the children, the elderly, the ill and the women go to this side.'

That side? There were trucks waiting there. I hear my father whispering to my mother, 'Fortunately there are trucks, how could I walk on the ice otherwise?'

The Germans separated the people who were supposed to get on the trucks.

After a while the officer in charge of our transport and an SS-man, approached us. They stopped my father, who was about to push us towards the crowd going to the trucks.

The SS-man asked him, 'Are you and your wife the ones who speak German?'

'Yes,' answered father and added, 'My children also speak very good German!'

The SS-man sized us up and asked sullenly, 'How old are they?'

This time father made us two to three years older, insisting, 'They are seventeen/eighteen.'

'Wait here until I come back,' the SS-man told us.

People continued to get into the trucks which, as soon as they were full, drove off. Where were they going? We had no idea!

How many tragic scenes remain unforgettable in my mind. Mothers whose children were taken away – running after them so that they wouldn't be separated. Old people calling to their child who remained behind. They snatched a young woman's baby by force and pushed her to the other side.

Screams, sobs, farewells. And the smartly dressed SS-men shouting and raging in their midst.

Suddenly all was silent. Nearly all the people were gone, only a few men and women remained. The SS-men formed them into columns, five abreast, men and women separated. They ordered them to march: '*Vorwärts! marsch! schneller! los!*' (Forward! March! Faster! Get moving!) We heard them shouting until we lost sight of them.

Only the four of us remained.

Everything had happened so quickly! All the people who got off the train had disappeared with the trucks. None of our traveling companions were there anymore, there was just us and some SS-men. The silence was overwhelming in the dark night. The spotlights that had turned night into day were switched off.

And we four were left standing there alone …

After some time a car with a Red Cross emblem finally stopped in front of us. 'Climb in,' an SS-man told us, and off we went.

'Coincidences' had saved us: all four of us spoke German, and because of my mother's despair we were in the first transport. What a coincidence it was that of the 2,800 people in the first transport, there was no one else who could speak German. And the Germans needed people to act as interpreters.

Fifty years later I reread facts the Germans themselves recorded. I feel the same terrible sense of resignation at this unbelievable, horrible, unheard-of event. The Germans wrote that on 20 March 1943 an RSHA (Reichssicherheitschauptamt, the Nazi Department of Security, organized in 1939) transport from Greece arrived. About 2,800 Jewish men, women and children from the Thessaloniki ghetto were on board. After the selection, 417 men were admitted to the camp (among them my father, who was given the number 109564, and my brother, who was given the number 109565) and 192 women (among them my mother, who was no. 38911, and myself, no. 38912).

These 609 men and women were admitted to the camp not to survive, but to live until they could endure no longer.

The rest of the '*persons*' – people like you and me, like your mother, your grandmother, your aunt, your father, your grandfather and your brothers and sisters – 2,191 people in all – a number reached by adding up individual '*human lives*' – were immediately trucked away and put to death in gas chambers.

And this was just the first transport from Greece – I am not talking about the others who came before us from all over Europe – and I am not talking about the remaining 15 transports that followed from the ghetto in Thessaloniki, with approximately the same number in each transport, until a total of 46,000 Thessalonikian Jews had arrived; – of whom 96 per cent were put to death upon arrival.

It is unimaginable, so frightening and inconceivable, so difficult to believe.

For the first time after many years I started to read more and more of the depositions of witnesses. I became outraged over and over again, as if I were not myself a former inmate of one of history's most terrible extermination camps.

And to top all those feelings, my exasperation flared up even more when I read the written orders of the SS and even more their reports, the photographs, the pedantically detailed records with all the details, many of which were saved despite the National Socialist's efforts to destroy all the evidence. Together with the survivors' testimonies there are documents that the SS did not destroy, preserving their orders, meetings, photographs and films.

A young schoolchild visited an exhibition organized in 1993 by the Jewish community of Thessaloniki, which included photographs and many objects connected with the Holocaust. He asked his father, full of astonishment: 'But were the Germans really stupid enough to keep all these records?'

It was around 2.30 or 3.00 a.m. when mother and I arrived at our destination. We had stopped on the way there, and my brother and father had disappeared in the custody of an SS-officer. I can still remember my father's look and feel his hand clasping mine before he climbed out. Where were they taking them? Would we see them again soon?

The car stopped in front of a big building. It was pitch dark all around us, a knock on the door, and a woman opened with a questioning expression. She wore a striped dress with a white kerchief on her head. She looked half asleep.

'Keep them here, they will stay for a few days until they are picked up,' said the SS-man who had accompanied us, and then he left.

The door closed and 'Maria' – that was her name – plied us with questions. 'Who are you? Where are you from? Why didn't they take you with the rest of them? How is it that you speak German? Who is protecting you?'

'Protecting' – I wondered what she meant?

My mother explained as best she could without herself knowing exactly what was happening.

After we had taken a shower, Maria took us into a room full of bunk beds – stacked one on top of the other, three levels high. Smoothly shaved heads like cabbages were visible everywhere.

Without thinking, I told my mother indignantly, 'Mama, they brought us here to the men.'

Maria corrected me, 'They are not men, they are women!'

After a six-day trip in the railroad car, sitting up the whole time, we were finally permitted to lie down. It seemed to me that I had slept for only five minutes when a very loud ringing woke us up.

It was 4.30 a.m. and around me I saw the women, whom I mistook for men when we arrived in the night, quickly getting ready.

Some of them bombarded us with questions. 'Why are you here?' – 'They brought you here straight from the station? – Unbelievable, this has never happened before – You did not go through delousing? – They did not cut your hair? – They did not tattoo your numbers on your arms? – But such a thing never happened before during the whole time the camp has been here! (Are you Jews? One hundred per cent? – And you did not bring a safe-conduct letter from any important person? – Unbelievable, unheard of!'

We asked who Maria was, and they told us that she was the *Blockälteste* – the block senior, a prisoner in charge of our barrack. Her full name was Maria Maul, a German Christian imprisoned for political reasons. 'And she is not bad!' they added.

We asked where were all the people had been taken who got into the trucks. For a moment dead silence reigned, a few women started to drift away from us, and two or three of them began to tell us the unbelievable, the unheard of: 'They don't exist any more, they burned them all, they are smoke rising from the smokestacks …'

Crazy, I thought, completely crazy! The poor fools don't know what they are saying! Bewildered, I heard Eva and Edith repeating this over and over, and then: '*Tschüss* – So long, we will see you again this evening, we can chat with you when we come back from work.'

We stayed on our own in the sleeping room, bewildered, speechless, terrified. There was no one else in the whole building except us, the *Blockälteste* Maria, and an SS-woman named Klaus. The latter was a very young and pretty woman. She was also amazed and kept on asking the same question: 'Do you have any special connections to be treated so differently?'

We didn't have any special connections, simply the 'coincidences' that saved us. We were the only Jews in the transport from Greece who could speak German. The SS desperately needed people who could interpret in order to communicate with inmates who spoke a language they didn't know and that was not at all like their own.

Our misfortune to be in the first transport was actually our good fortune. Thanks to a coincidence we had been spared the first experience, the terrible shock that all the newcomers went through when they entered the camp gates.

How lucky we were – to this day I can hardly believe it.

Sarika described to me her first shock three days later when they took my mother and me to Birkenau concentration camp to cut our hair, tattoo a number on our left arm and bring us to the barrack housing the office of the 'Political Department' (Politische Abteilung or 'PA'), the camp Gestapo, where we were to work as translators and interpreters.

When they were led away from the station, the girls had to walk in the cold, the coldest night of their lives, to a large barrack – the delousing block. 'We were shaking,' she told me, 'from the cold, the frost, the hardship, hunger and the terrible fear that had taken hold of us. They ordered us to undress and to wait. To wait for what? For how long? How embarrassed I felt standing stark naked while the SS-men walked around us, how humiliating, how degrading!'

'After a long time, it seemed to me like years, we proceeded to a room where women prisoners in striped outfits were cutting our hair with quick, clumsy, abrupt movements. Every so often SS voices sounded: '*Schnell! Schnell!*' (Faster! Faster!) You could hear the clip-clip of the scissors. We did not recognize ourselves. Our heads were as bald as cabbages. On the floor were piles of hair, braids, curls of all colors. We looked at each other in despair and didn't recognize each other. Leah broke into hysterical laughter. Allegrita couldn't bear it anymore, she started crying and called out for her mother. One crack of an SS whip and they all fell silent. Allegrita collapsed on the floor. They took us to the showers. At the entrance they gave us a rock-hard piece of soap to wash with. The water alternated between boiling hot and ice cold, and the SS yelled: '*Los! Los!*' (Come on! Come on!)

Then, after registration and receiving a serial number, their number was tattooed on to their left arm. Now they were all numbers in the concentration camp. Who knew for how long?

Sarika hurriedly told me all this, her voice despairing, in a corner of a latrine where we accidentally met. She also told me that she was supposed to work in the 'Aussenkommando' (labor detachments which worked outside the camp), though she didn't know what that meant. She asked anxiously if I knew where her parents had been taken – knowing no foreign language, she could not communicate with anybody and didn't know anything about their fate. What could I tell her? Why should I add to her despair?

'They are fine, don't worry,' I told her. We arranged to meet again in the toilets whenever we could.

Already on this first day in Auschwitz we learned all the details about what exactly an extermination camp was. The information the girls gave us before they went to work was supplemented by Maria, our *Blockälteste*, as we helped her with her chores. She told us about the gas chambers, about the crematoria where they burned the corpses so nothing would remain. She told us about the selections that were made twice a day, every day, she told us …

'But this is insane,' I thought, 'she is talking nonsense in such a matter-of-fact tone, and we are listening to her?' I did not believe her until I had experienced and seen everything with my own eyes.

Sometime later Klaus, the SS-overseer, came into the room and we immediately stopped talking. Suddenly, Klaus called me over to her and hastily ordered: 'Lift your dress up quickly, I want to see your tail.'

My tail? What tail? What is she talking about? But she was quite serious and meant what she said. She had been brainwashed by Hitler's anti-Semitic propaganda – one of the many things he had said was that Jews were all the Devil's instruments and had tails …

The next day they picked us up and transferred us to Auschwitz II – Birkenau. There they cut off our hair, tattooed numbers on our arms and gave us the striped outfits that all prisoners wore.

On the left side of our 'dress' we had to sew the number they gave us printed on a white strip of fabric. On the right side we wore two triangles, a yellow one and a red one, one on top of the other, forming a star of David. In the middle of the star was printed a letter 'G' for Greece.

Men and women had their numbers sewn on their clothes. The Christian 'political prisoners' wore only a single red triangle. If they were not 'political' prisoners, they wore 'angles' of a different color, green for criminals, pink for homosexuals, black for 'asocial persons', purple for Jehovah's Witnesses. In this way we knew immediately how each prisoner was classified by the Nazis.

The living conditions in Birkenau were appalling. There was an endless plot of land with a row of identical wood barracks, the so-called 'blocks' where the prisoners lived as long as they survived. Inside there were the three-level '*Kojen*', as they called our bunk beds. They were wide enough for three or four people, but there were never less than eight or ten people in them. On the top of the slats were straw-filled sacks intended to serve as 'mattresses' and two or three thread-bare, lice-infested wool blankets.

We lay next to each other, all facing the same way, and when someone wanted to turn over, we all had to turn together. Cold penetrated from all sides, and although there was something resembling a heater in the room, we were always cold. Next to the entrance there was a little room containing the office and the *Blockälteste*'s bed. During my entire stay in Birkenau I slept in that same block.

Every night before we went to bed we examined our clothes for lice. We sat half-naked in the freezing room, huddled on our 'beds', searching the seams of our clothes for lice. Then, pressed against each other to keep warm, we tried to sleep.

Next to me was a Jewish girl from Holland. She was so miserable, so desperate. She was afraid of morning. The thought that on the coming day she would again have to carry stones in the freezing weather, painfully starving, was unbearable to her. 'I don't think I will last one more day,' she told me. So the night went by – ever so fast.

Every day, early at dawn, they woke us up with bells and wild shouting. '*Schnell! Anziehen!*' (Quick! Get dressed! Come out for the *Appell* [the roll call].) Without anything warm to drink, still half asleep, we had to get out in the cold and stand in rows until the SS and the person in charge of the block – the *Blockälteste* – came and counted us.

The SS-men came half-an-hour later, wearing warm winter coats and holding dogs on leashes. The *Blockälteste* had to stand at attention in front of them and report the number of prisoners. Then, with an air of superiority and hardness, the SS walked up and down counting us. We stood at attention, motionless, waiting. If the number was correct, everything was in order and we could return to our block.

But most of the time something was not in order. Prisoners often died during the night and no one noticed. During the wake-up there was so much commotion, and everything had to be done so quickly that each of us was only concerned to get ready and get out, because if she delayed, she risked being beaten.

When the right number of prisoners were not present at roll call, the block would be searched until they found the inmate who had died or was too ill to get up. The *Appell* lasted for hours. What a torture and how many of us couldn't hold out! All of a sudden there would be a 'thump', and a girl had collapsed on the ground. The roll call was held each day, rain or snow.

Many girls, unable to endure this any longer, ended their own lives. They would throw themselves against the electric fences, and in the morning they were found dead, their flesh burned to the wires.

Our outfits were made of a coarse cloth with wide blue-and-gray stripes. Instead of warming us, we felt even colder in them! We wore kerchiefs on our shaved heads. Our shoes were wooden clogs, and we were among the lucky ones who had socks to wear. That was the uniform of the prisoners who worked 'under a roof'.

All the other women wore either striped outfits or any

other worn-out and useless discards they were given. If they were lucky, they were given socks for their frozen feet, otherwise they put their bare feet in the wooden clogs. If they were unlucky enough to lose their clogs, they would walk barefoot in the mud. The entire grounds of the camp were covered with mud up to our ankles. The lucky women wore kerchiefs on their heads.

A picture of Birkenau as it was then still haunts my dreams at night. During the day 'ghosts' in the form of women slipped about in the fog, the rain, the snow. Around their waists was a cord from which their *Menage* hung, a deep pot with two handles. It was their most precious possession. Without this utensil they would die of hunger even faster. Only those who had a *Menage* were given the watery broth which was ladled out as a meal once a day. As soon as they received their 'soup' they immediately sat down on the ground on one side and, holding it with hands trembling from cold and exhaustion, sipped it as best as they could. After that they continued their aimless pacing, up and down, apathetic, eyes filled with despair, staring without seeing, abandoned in their thoughts without any will at all to make the least effort to survive. What for? Why?

Very often an SS-man or woman would pass by, always with a dog, and for no good reason they would curse and whip these ill-fated creatures. There were 'newcomers' who had not been allocated a job yet. Others worked under a *Kapo*'s supervision. Their job was to carry stones from one spot to another for no purpose at all. An SS-woman with a dog oversaw the 'work' from nearby, and if she didn't like something – this happened continually – she would start yelling at them and let her dog loose on them. Others had to drag big iron rollers, the kind used to flatten the ground. A great iron bar was mounted like a shaft on each roller, and from eight to ten girls had to pull together, as they could be moved only with great effort. There were also the unspecialized newcomers who worked in the Aussenkommando.

Every day after roll call – the *Appell* – each detachment's *Kapo* would assemble the women in uniform rows of five and then they were ready to pass through the big gates of the camp. On the left side of the gate the camp 'orchestra' stood and played military marches until all the prisoners had passed through. The 'orchestra' was made up of prisoners; the lucky ones who knew how to play an instrument were chosen with great care. For a while, Dr Menashé's daughter played in the orchestra.

On the other side stood the camp's chief physician, Dr Rohde. Next to him stood the two chief SS-women in charge, Drechsler and Mandel. Dr Rohde, and in his absence Drechsler, made selections by pointing with a finger at the thinnest, palest and most terrified prisoners, who were sent to Block 25 and from there to the gas chambers. An additional selection took place late in the afternoon at the return from work. The orchestra played on one side, and the SS people selected, moving only a finger. And this happened, without fail, morning and evening until 18 January 1945, the day when the evacuation of Auschwitz began.

'One week long, twice every day I passed through this selection,' Esterina told me. 'As soon as I was close to the gate, I would raise my head, look straight ahead and try to walk confidently in my ungainly clogs, trying to deceive them so they wouldn't see the big boils on my feet!' She managed to do this until, to her great good fortune, they transferred her to the 'Schuh-Kommando' – shoe detachment. Then she didn't have to go through the twice-daily selection, because she worked in the camp 'under a roof'.

After our hair had been shaved off and a number tattooed on our arms, they led us to a barrack, a 'block', where we were to work in the future. That was the office of the Politische Abteilung (PA), the camp Gestapo, the SS.

The Politische Abteilung was the most important office the Germans had in the camp. All the orders for the camp were sent there and then passed on. That is where they kept detailed records of all the events that happened every day everywhere in the Auschwitz and Birkenau camps. That is where they kept all the lists with the names of the people who had passed the selection and those who would be sent to the gas chambers. All the orders from the RSHA, all orders for executions, all interrogations, everything was steered from the Politische Abteilung.

In order to run the camp administration, the SS employed mostly women prisoners and a few men as 'personnel'. The PA prisoners' *Kommando* was divided into the following groups: the Document Section, the Interrogation Section, the Legal Section and the 'Standesamt', the recorder's office, including the civil registry, and the 'administration' and 'management' of the crematoria.

Lore Shelley called her book about the prisoners who worked in the Politische Abteilung *Secretaries of Death* (New York: Shengold, 1986), because it was well known that anyone who worked in this *Kommando* or in the Sonderkommando for the crematoria would never leave the camp alive. Not because of hardship or hunger, but because they were the most important witnesses to the German crimes. This is the reason why they regularly replaced the people working in these *Kommandos*. They killed them in the gas chambers and then replaced them so there would be no witnesses.

My mother's job was to write the newcomers' personal facts on a specially printed form, i.e., the name and surname of each prisoner. Every time she wrote a name on the special forms, Sarah had to be written next to a woman's name, Israel next to a man's name.

In the Auschwitz museum the printed forms have been preserved with my brother's and cousin Emilia's names written on 20 March 1943. Although the SS destroyed many documents before they abandoned the camp to the Russians, they didn't succeed in destroying everything and making every document disappear as they wanted to. By another 'coincidence', my brother's and my cousin's forms were among those not destroyed.

I usually went to any of the secretaries who needed me to act as an interpreter. The transports from Greece arrived one after the other. How many times there were relatives, friends and acquaintances on them! Everybody without fail asked me, 'Where did they take our parents? Why did they separate us?'

I can still hear my mother's set reply: 'They are fine, don't worry about them, do the best you can to survive, this is your duty.'

I never saw Sarika again. A few days later I read her name on the list of Block 25, the death block. My colleague Edith typed all the names on a typewriter. That was when I burst into sobs for the first time since our deportation, and the last time for many years.

A woman in one of the transports that arrived around the middle of May told my mother that she had come in the same railroad car as my grandfather. Full of anguish, mother asked if he had been admitted to the camp. 'No, he was taken away in a truck, I don't know where they took him … Do you know, Mrs Kounio, where they took him?'

Did she know! Full of grief, mother and I wondered how he had been captured? He was so well-hidden, was it possible that the people who hid him had betrayed him? Questions that were only answered after the liberation.

Someone who had worked as an interpreter for the Gestapo in Thessaloniki told us that grandfather had been well-hidden and that he could have survived. What happened was that grandfather still believed in the German people. He felt so lonely away from his family that one Sunday morning he took all the decorations he had earned as a Captain during the First World War, along with his diploma and went to the Gestapo.

Extremely politely, the witness recounted, the SS received him and asked who he was and what he wanted.

'I am Dr of Engineering Ernst Loevy, and these are my identification papers.'

He showed them what he had bought with him.

'And what do you want?' the SS-man asked him.

'To be sent to where my daughter and her family went.'

The SS-officer put a junior officer in charge, instructing him, 'Please lead Dr Ernst Loevy to the station. From there in a few days he will have the opportunity to join his daughter.'

Surely our intelligent, kindly, but so very innocent grandfather must have thought how very civilized the Germans were at the office, exactly as he had expected. Did he realize what had happened to him as he was led, together with others, to the gas chambers?

We did not know anything yet about the fate of my father and brother. We were filled with anguish.

Our work in the PA went on non-stop, because an uninterrupted string of transports was arriving from Greece. Our supervisor was SS-Unterscharführer (Corporal) Klauss, known for his cruelty and hatred of Jews. His own colleagues called him *'Der Judenfresser'* – 'devourer of Jews'.

One of the SS-men was a good artist, and to pass his time he would sketch all his colleagues in characteristic scenes from daily life. He drew SS-Corporal Klauss, the cruel man who hated Jews, standing, legs spread, in front of an open crematorium door from which flames were bursting forth. Thick smoke spewed out of a great smokestack. In the smoke he drew Stars of David. In his hand Klauss held a huge shovel full of corpses, ready to throw them into the flames.

That was Klauss. Nevertheless, this bestial man was our link to my father. He went almost daily from Birkenau to Auschwitz, and many times to the camp's laundry, since according to my mother he was the director of the laundry. He was always very good to us and showed us particular affection, perhaps because he himself came from Karlsbad.

One day when he was leaving for the other camp I asked him if he could find out something about my father and brother. He looked at me sullenly and did not answer. However, when he came back, he snapped at my mother,

'Your husband and son are fine! They are working in the camp tailor shop. I told them that you are fine too …' During the time I worked in Birkenau Klauss also brought us news on two other occasions.

One day, as I was going from my 'service' barrack to the toilet, I saw an SS-woman setting her dog loose on a girl; the dog lunged at her. I thought it was Oriko, with whom I had made the train trip to the camp, and I instinctively wanted to run to her aid. Suddenly I felt someone holding me back with great force. It was one of my co-workers, a Czechoslovakian girl named Edith Winter. She dragged me back to the offices. If Edith, who immediately grasped what I was about to do, had not been there, I might not be alive today.

The toilets we used were off-limits to the other women prisoners, especially to the newcomers, for whom there was a pit somewhere on one side of the camp. Only the ones who worked in a regular *Kommando* and the Christian inmates were authorized to use our toilets. It was a big room, with rude 'benches' on the left and right sides, and holes one next to the other where we sat to relieve ourselves.

Prisoners who had reached the most miserable stage – the last stage of their lives – were known as *Muselmänner* (the walking dead). Where this name came from and what it meant I still don't know even today. The fact is that they were usually reduced to this state within only a short time after their arrival. One or two weeks was long enough.

One day when I was in the toilet, a *Muselweib* (one of these wretched women) dared to enter and sit down. Unfortunately for her one of the women who wore a green triangle next to her number was passing by and looked in. 'What are you doing here?' she yelled and gave her a push which knocked her into the pit, and then she left! Together with two others who happened to be there, we pulled the unfortunate woman out in a sorry state. I wonder even now what she did after she got out, how she cleaned herself up, whether she survived?

Besides the hunger and lack of basic hygiene, the sores on

our feet from wearing the wooden clogs and the lice that tortured us, we were all plagued by diarrhea.

After work we would come back to our blocks. They gave us a watery 'soup', in which potato peels floated, and a piece of bread. That had to last until noon the next day. Many had the courage not to eat all the bread in the evening and saved half of it for the morning. Bread and clogs were placed under their pillows, well-guarded so they wouldn't be stolen.

How easily people's characters change! Who would have thought that one miserable woman would steal bread from another miserable woman? But often at dawn many would discover that their bread or clogs had been stolen in the night and then start shrieking and yelling in despair.

Throughout the whole period when transports were arriving from Greece, we were given olives with our food. The SS-people, unaccustomed to their taste, didn't want to eat the olives, so they gave them to the prisoners. Many times even the prisoners couldn't eat them, and then they gave them to us. How tasty they were …

The transports from Greece arrived one after the other every two or three days. Then we had to work constantly until late, until we were finished registering the new arrivals. There were about ten clerks, if I am not mistaken. Most of the girls came from Czechoslovakia and had arrived before us. They were chosen for this work because they had experience in secretarial work and typing and spoke German. They were among the lucky ones who, because of their knowledge and skills, managed to survive. I was the youngest one there and they all tried to help me and hide my mistakes. I tried to understand what they were saying, but although my German was fairly good I didn't always understand. SS-man Klauss often pretended not to notice my mistakes.

Not long after we were sent to Birkenau, I think four or five weeks, I became very ill. For two or three days I went to work with an unbearable headache and high temperature. I was afraid to say anything, and my mother felt the same. Again, luck was with me. SS-man Klauss gave orders for me to be admitted to the *Revier* (camp infirmary). It was a barrack with lines of beds, one next to the other. They were arranged in rows of two three-level bunk beds separated by a very narrow aisle. The whole place smelled strongly of disinfectant. There were virtually no medications, but they tried to keep the place clean. The most important thing was that one could sleep all day long. The hospital was intended chiefly for Christian prisoners, but for an inexplicable reason they sometimes sent Jews there as well. Every so often the SS-doctor went through and 'cleansed' the ward of its Jewish patients.

In the *Revier*'s book, where they wrote my name and number, they stated that I had '*Kopfgrippe*' – flu.

In charge of the *Revier* was a woman doctor, a Christian 'political prisoner' from Poland. Her assistant was Dr Ena, a Jewish woman doctor from Czechoslovakia. They decided that they would hide and protect me from the frequent selections. Therefore they assigned me to a bed close to the wall, high up on the third level. They put me next to a Polish countess who had been arrested a year before because she was an active member of the Polish resistance. She was a very beautiful woman. I was impressed by her number, which was very low, and by the big red triangle sewn on her blouse. She lay like a shield in front of me, hiding me every time an SS-doctor passed by.

Next to my head on the one side was a bedpan in which I could relieve myself. On the other side of my head Dr Ena placed a dish of water and a 'cloth' to moisten my forehead. I suffered from terrible headaches and my whole body was in pain. I was in a state of constant numbness. Sometimes I could hear my mother's voice as she applied a fresh cloth to my forehead. I was thirsty, very thirsty. I dreamed of my father coming home from work carrying a big paper bag full of oranges, as he used to do when we lived at home. Every so often I would dream of the watermelon split open on the floor in Vozio's basement and craved another piece. Sometimes I imagined myself at home, on the platform gazing at my beloved sea.

For three whole weeks I lay in a state of continuous delirium. My strong constitution and 'will to live' were what kept me alive, as Dr Ena told my mother.

One day, when I was starting to recover, the camp's chief doctor, Dr Rohde, came for an inspection, accompanied by the SS-woman in charge of the women's camp, named Drechsler. Drechsler and her colleague Mandel (at the time 23 years old; cf. D. Czech 'A Calendar of Events in the Concentration Camps of Auschwitz and Birkenau, 1939–1945', Rowohlt, 1989, pp. 316 ff) competed with each other to see who could be more cruel and inhumane. Dr Rohde was famous for his calm, serious expression as he inspected the lines of prisoners on their way to work. On that day Rohde and Drechsler went from room to room, and the two prisoner physicians followed in their wake. All the patients had to come down from their beds and stand in line at attention.

The ever-so-dignified Dr Rohde walked along the aisle, always carrying a whip in his hand, as all the SS-people did, and every so often he pointed at a girl, who then had to leave the line and go to the other side.

When he arrived in front of me, he sized me up from head to toe and asked: 'What's wrong with you?' In my innocence, I replied: 'Typhus.' From behind his back I could see Dr Ena uttering a silent 'Oh!' and putting her hand over her mouth. The SS-doctor turned around and looked at her, petrified as she was, and I heard Dr Ena saying hurriedly: '*Kopfgrippe*, Herr Uberführer' (Flu, First Lieutenant, Sir). He turned around, scrutinized me thoroughly and then continued his inspection.

This was one of the coincidences that saved my life. Another was that the Polish countess with whom I shared a bed received small food parcels from her people. (She had this privilege because she was a political prisoner.) For a whole week while I was at the *Revier* she shared her food with me and this helped me to recover even faster.

Then it was back to work at the PA.

Very close to the PA offices was Block 25. This was a barrack where they detained the people singled out at a selection. They often held them there for three or four days before sending them to the gas chambers. About this time another big 'selection' was made, as happened whenever the camp got overcrowded.

Turmoil prevailed in our offices! The lists with all the names of the prisoners sent to Block 25 had to be completed quickly, and the names had to be written rapidly and correctly. The SS-people breathed down our necks so there wouldn't be any interruption, any delay. We typed until late in the night and one could hear the clack, clack, clack of the typewriters for hours on end.

This is another sign of the pedantic nature of the Germans in charge. Lists of the 'candidates for death' had to be drawn up accurately and filed in an archive. This name registration took place after every selection, whether it was one of the mass selections, as in this case, or the daily ones held every morning when the prisoners went to work and every evening when they returned.

The RSHA arrivals became even more frequent and the gas chambers and crematoria lacked sufficient capacity.

Our *Kommando* also included the Politische Abteilung messengers, '*Laüferinnen*', as they were called. Their job was to bring orders, lists and messages from one camp to the other. From them we learned the news of the other camp and sometimes news of the outside world. Most of them were involved in the camp's Polish resistance, and in this way they were able to enter all the offices and talk to the men who worked there. Most of them were Polish Christians and were perceived as the camp's elite.

One of the messengers was Mala, known by all for her

courage, beauty and good nature. She was Belgian, very well-educated and spoke several languages. I admired and liked her very much. Sometimes, when she was not pressed for time as she usually was, she would talk to me and she would say: 'Courage little one, one day this nightmare will be over.' One day she shocked us with the news that four new crematoria had been built in Birkenau and were now ready to operate. We were overcome by anxiety about what the future would bring.

4 • *Bookkeeper of Death in Auschwitz*

On 8 June 1943 the last transport arrived from Thessaloniki. Our presence was no longer necessary in Birkenau. They needed us in the central offices.

It must have been the end of June 1943 when they transferred us, my mother and me, back to Auschwitz, which was mainly a men's camp. The men's camp was different from Birkenau. There was a row of houses, former barracks built of red bricks with red roofs. The entrance was a large gate with an arch over it proclaiming the camp motto, '*Arbeit Macht Frei*' (work makes you free), in big letters. On the left and the right stood guard towers.

The camp was entirely surrounded by a double row of electrified fences. Located at regular intervals were guard towers, from which SS-men watched the camp grounds. They also had powerful spotlights that rotated to the left and the right to illuminate the camp.

Outside the men's camp, not far from the gate, stood another building with its own electrified fence. That building was called the '*Stabsgebäude*', the staff building. It housed about 300 women who worked for the SS, just as we had worked in the PA. There must have been about 65 women in our *Kommando*. The building also housed a *Wäscherei* (laundry for SS clothing), a tailor shop, where their uniforms were repaired, and more. There must have been, as I said above, around 300 women who both worked and slept there.

The living conditions in the *Stabsgebäude* were totally different from those in Birkenau. The sleeping rooms also had three-level bunk beds, one next to the other, but we each had our own bed. The main thing was that it was clean, that we could wash and that we were fed regular, though unappetizing, meals.

Aside from the SS, the person in charge of cleanliness and the orderly management of the building was Maria, the *Blockälteste*. As I said earlier, she was the one who had received us when we arrived in Auschwitz. Maria was a kind-hearted woman who always spoke to us in a considerate tone, and often she spent the night comforting women who had awakened screaming because of nightmares.

Our clothes always had to be clean and tidy. We wore the official camp uniform: dresses with wide blue-and-gray stripes with our number written on the left side. We had white kerchiefs on our shaved heads. Thus the SS always had clean, presentable prisoners around them.

In order to protect their health, the SS demanded cleanliness from the prisoners who came into contact with them, and the 'faultless appearance of their clothes!'

We nicknamed our *Kommando* the 'Himmelfahrts-kommando', which means the 'Ascension Detachment', because we were certain we would never leave the camp alive. This was not because of hardship or hunger, but because of our work. We were important witnesses, just like those in the Sonderkommando (who worked in the gas chambers). Besides, the SS and our bosses never missed the opportunity to remind us that there was only one way out for us: 'Through the gas chamber and the smokestack.'

They put my mother and me to work in the 'Todesabteilung' (section of the dead). This section's job was, from day to day, to prepare death-certificates for deceased male and female prisoners who had not come to the camp on the RSHA trains, as we had, but rather from prisons or who had been captured in raids, and also for those who died in the camp from hunger, hardship, typhus, beatings, torture and so on.

But especially for those who had not entered the camp through the RSHA, a death-certificate had to be issued stating as the cause of death something suggestive of death from natural causes, such as cardiac arrest or a kidney infection, etc. For prisoners the SS killed for fun or amusement, or other reasons, the death-certificate would list as the cause of death '*Auf der Flucht gestorben*', which meant they had died while trying to escape.

Every time a Christian died, a 'letter' was sent to the family expressing the administration's condolences and stating the cause of death. Each letter ended with a postscript asking if the relatives would like to receive the ashes of the deceased, and if so, to send a certain amount of marks to cover the costs.

This was my mother's job. We also had to separate the files of the people who died and bring them down from the top floor, the section of the living, to the basement, the 'Todesabteilung'.

The names of all the people selected in the Birkenau and Auschwitz camps were written on lists sent to the central office of the PA, where we worked, for registration. On each of those lists were the identifying letters SB which stood for '*Sonderbehandlung*' (special treatment).

The people on the SB lists had received 'special treatment', in other words they had been killed in the gas chambers. We all knew the significance of SB. 'Under no circumstances were we allowed to admit our knowledge of the meaning of SB, a euphemism the SS kept secret,' writes Lore Shelley in her book *Secretaries of Death* (New York: Shengold, 1986, p. 9 f.).

> Once, one of us by mistake said, 'Herr Unterscharführer [corporal], this man belongs to the dead of the S.B.' The Unterscharführer stared at her piercingly from head to toe. 'Are you crazy? Who says that the man is dead? This man is not dead, he is S.B. – don't forget this!"
>
> Another time an SS officer from a different section visited the card file department and asked for the meaning of the letters S.B. A woman of our Kommando told him she did not know. 'How come you don't know if you are working here?' 'I only do what I am told to do,' she replied. 'Well, we'll see,' the officer said and called

> the head of the office, Oberscharführer Kirschner. Pointing to the prisoner, he declared, 'She does not know the meaning of S.B. She does not know that her own file will one day also carry the remark, S.B.,' and both started to roar with laughter.

I was present during the episode Lore Shelley describes in her book. I was putting away the files, one of the jobs I was assigned to do. I was responsible for filing all the dead inmates' files in alphabetical order and for filing the SB lists which came in daily. They gave me those jobs because they were easy and did not require any special knowledge of German.

In our office big cabinets lined the walls. In them, suspended in horizontal rows of four, were all the folders for prisoners who came from other camps. I was responsible for looking after them, making sure they were in the correct order, looking for the folders that were requested and, when files were returned, putting them back in their place. On the cover of each folder, on the bottom right corner, was the prisoner's number. These were special folders with a spring-like hanger so they could be hung in the cabinet like clothes. They were arranged according to serial numbers. Most of them were large, very thick volumes containing all the official documents of the prisons and the prisoners' previous records, which accompanied them to every prison and were updated after every interrogation. Why was someone arrested, what had he done, how had he been arrested, whether he had been tortured and what he had revealed. Many times they would write on the file remarks such as: '*Rückkehr unerwünscht*' (return not desired) or '*Standesgerichtssache*' (registry court matter) or '*Waffenbesitz*' (possession of weapons), etc. A file could contain an entire life-story, starting long before a prisoner was arrested and ending on the day he was transferred to Auschwitz concentration camp.

Often I was alone in the office and had some free time. I

would open one of the files and avidly read through it. The supervisor of our department knew about this and always protected me. My curiosity drove me to read more and more, and many times I would even creep into the cabinet to read in peace and quiet.

First I read my Polish colleagues' files, they were all political prisoners and had been held in Auschwitz since 1940. This is the reason why their numbers were so low, like Feliks Mylyk: No. 92, one of the first prisoners in Auschwitz when it was opened in 1940. [According to a letter from Wilibald Pajak to Erika Kounio-Amariglio of 26 February 1996, 'Feliks' Mylyk died in 1994.] Marian Gemsky, No. 485 was another of my colleagues [Wilibald Pajak gives his real name as Jan Gemczyk, transferred to Buchenwald concentration camp (near Weimar) in 1944 and shot there in January or February 1945 for 'plundering'] and Willy [Wilibald] Pajak [according to his letter he became the block secretary in Block 16a in April, 1944], with whom I worked in the same section, the 'Todesabteilung'.

These were our three male 'colleagues', and although we all worked in the same room, we were not allowed to talk to each other. If we had to ask them anything relevant to our jobs, the ever-present SS-man had to act as intermediary. This was the rule. Despite that, during the months and years we spent working together we were able to find ways to exchange words, to indicate anything that attracted our attention, and to comment on it.

I read *Blockälteste* Maria's file. My admiration was great for these people who became my heroes because of all they had done and suffered.

I also read the files of those who had a black, green or pink triangle, and often I was horrified by what they had done. Naturally it terrified me to read these accounts, but my colleagues helped me a lot. Whenever a prisoner died, I had to remove his folder and bring it to the basement, but never did so before I had read it from start to finish.

Fifty years later I am still trying to understand what exactly we did in the PA offices. During my imprisonment in the camp I worked there without ever really understanding the things that were happening around me.

In 1986 my fellow prisoner Lore Shelley interviewed all the survivors of our *Kommando* who wanted to tell about their experiences and their job for the camp's Gestapo. Her book, *Secretaries of Death*, is very enlightening. Various events come back to my mind as I read it. All the pieces now fit into the right place like a puzzle, and my astonishment is even greater at the perfect operation of the SS bureaucracy, its ability to record everything in the smallest detail. How can I understand anybody who believes that all our stories are figments of our imaginations? Despite the attempts by the SS to destroy anything they put down in writing, not everything has been lost, and documents are available to everybody who wants to study them, in the Auschwitz museum, in Yad Va'shem, and in other archives.

How could I not repeat that it was a 'coincidence' that we survived, when the fact was that those working in such 'important' positions as ours were merely living 'on borrowed time'?

But let me return to 50 years ago. One day – it must have been the middle of July 1943, I don't remember exactly – they called me to the office of SS-man Perry Broad to work as an interpreter. There was a prisoner there in bad shape, a real *Muselmänn*. He was wearing a prisoner's striped outfit, and in his hand he was nervously clutching the cap that all male prisoners wore. He was in a frantic state and was talking loudly in Greek. He talked so fast and was so out of breath that at first I could not understand him. Tears were streaming from his eyes. What had happened?

He tried to explain to the SS-man that he was not Jewish, that he was on the train with the Jews by mistake. He had formerly sold *koulouria*, round bread sticks, at the station whenever a transport train departed. He had done this many times and always returned home afterward. But the last time he was swept along by the crowd, and the Germans, as he said, shoved and forced people to walk even faster. He could not go back or leave and was carried along by the crowd, and together with everybody else he was forced on to the train.

When he arrived in the camp, he tried to explain that he was not a Jew and that they should let him go. Nobody could understand what he was talking about and even if they could they would have done the same to him, because he had come with the RSHA dispatch. So they tattooed a number on his arm, putting the yellow triangle over the red as they characteristically did to all the Jews. Together with everybody else he was admitted to the camp.

'Explain to them,' he was saying, 'you understand that I am not Jewish, I want them to understand this, too. Here, I will take off my trousers to show them that I was never circumcised.' And he tried to lower his trousers, but an SS-man behind him did not permit this. I tried to explain that he definitely was not Jewish. 'I can tell from his accent,' I told them. The SS-man listened indifferently without saying a word, and at a certain moment the desolate 'bread-stick' man tried to detach the number from his jacket, pleading in sobs: 'Tell them to change my number, to take the yellow triangle off the top so that at least I will not have to go through selection every day.'

The Germans did not let him continue speaking. They grabbed him and threw him outside. I returned to my work. I don't know what happened to him, but I am sure he did not survive. I have never forgotten him to this day, and every time I remember him tears come to my eyes and I feel a lump in my throat.

There was never a day in our offices when something upsetting did not happen. Every time the messengers came they had something terrible to announce that had happened in Birkenau camp. Lists from the men's camps at Auschwitz and Birkenau arrived regularly, as did ones from the women's camp, from Block 25 at Birkenau. We all tried to look at the names to see if any of our acquaintances' names were on the lists. Sometimes we would hear that someone had managed to escape. Our hearts rejoiced, and we prayed that they wouldn't be caught.

Once, to our great anxiety, they carried out a selection of thousands of Jewish prisoners who were in a bad state. The camp was again overcrowded, and space had to be freed for the Jews who kept arriving in thousands every day. We worked steadily until late in the night for nervous, angry SS-men who spurred us on: faster, faster! The head man, SS-Oberscharführer (Staff-Sergeant) Kirschner, whom we all feared, screamed about every little thing, and he got angry at his secretary, a prisoner who was also in charge of our *Kommando*, Edith Grünwald. The poor woman, pale with her eyes bulging, got angry at us in turn.

After one such *razzia* (police raid) in the women's camp at Birkenau, I found the names of my dear classmates Dorin Kovo and Rita Saltiel while reading the lists. Fifty years later, even today I feel my heart contract, and the same sob I felt then sticks in my throat.

Over the grapevine, news of the war sometimes penetrated into the camp – even that the Germans were starting to lose. Suddenly a ray of hope would light up our hearts, only to dim again the next day.

The PA building where we worked was outside the barbed wire of the men's camp. It was exactly opposite Block 1 in the men's camp. This building was the block where the men from the Schneirei-Kommando slept – the tailors. My father and brother worked there. Men who worked in the PA office of 'Auschwitz I' used to come to our office frequently. This made it possible for us to send messages to my father and receive his in return.

One day a 'colleague' told us that at a certain time my father would leave the block and try to stand on the steps before continuing on his way to work. Maybe he could see us, or we could see him?

From our toilet window we could see Block 1 in the men's camp. Of course there was a double line of barbed wire separating us. At the appointed time I climbed on to a toilet seat and managed to catch sight, just for a moment, of my father, who was coming out of the building. He turned his head towards our building and briefly stopped ... and then he went on. The sight of my father dressed in the striped camp uniform, a cap on his shaved head, looking so thin and haggard with his big eyes, still makes my heart ache, just as it did then. He could not see us.

After that we caught glimpses of him several times more. The girls knew about it and were on guard. Sometimes either my mother or myself would go outside, and we would stand for seconds gazing across the barbed wire. One day an SS-man entered the latrine just when I was standing on the toilet seat. 'My God! What will happen now,' I worried, terrified. I pretended to be fixing the water cistern, shaking all over. He left without saying a word! I never found out if he knew what I was doing up there, or why he came into our toilets.

A few days later my mother went down with typhoid fever and was sent to the *Revier* (infimary) in Birkenau. This was a terrible shock for me. I was filled with anxiety. Had they taken her to the *Revier* or to Block 25? I learned from Mala that they had indeed taken her to the infirmary. Dr Ena was looking after her as best she could, just as she had done for me. She even took her outside the barrack to sit in the sun for warmth. Cousin Rosa saw her there by chance and told my other cousin, Emilia, and both went to visit her. They were both in a wretched state, my mother told me. She promised to do whatever she could to bring them closer to us, if she returned to Auschwitz.

A few weeks later my mother did return to Auschwitz. She was now a real *Muselweib*, a shadow of her old self. She spoke to me constantly about the two girls, my cousins.

About that time the word went around in our block that more personnel were needed at the *Nähstube*, the tailor shop where the girls worked, sewing and repairing SS clothing. With the help of *Blockälteste* Maria and SS-woman Volkenrath, the names of Emilia and Rosa, as well as that of my dear friend May Benroubi, were added to the list. Unfortunately, Rosa had died in the meantime, and May was in Block 25, where there was no chance of ever leaving alive. Only our Emilia came. She was the fifth member of our family who was saved. The rest, 23 people, did not survive.

SS-woman Volkenrath had apparently been a clerk at the German Embassy in Paris. According to what she told my mother, with whom she had a friendly relationship, they had asked her to serve her country in a more substantial way. So they transferred her to Auschwitz. She told my mother that she had never heard of Auschwitz before and that it was a big surprise for her.

My mother was slowly starting to recover when she suddenly started having terrible headaches. She continued to work despite the agonizing pain, however. She was afraid to talk about it for fear of being sent back to Birkenau. The girls often hid her because she could not work and did her work for her. The image that I have kept in my memory ever since then is of how she held her head in her hands, as if she were holding it so it wouldn't burst. I don't remember how it happened, but one of the SS-people in charge saw how much she was suffering and sent her to be examined at the medical office of the men's camp, accompanied by an SS-officer.

A Polish prisoner was the physician there, a Dr Vasilevsky. After he examined her, he told her she had mastoiditis. He simply had to operate on the abscess – there was no alternative. He explained to her what he was going to do and asked her if she could bear the pain without making a sound, because he had no anaesthetic except for some strong red wine. 'Woe to both of us if you cry out,' he warned her, 'because they would discover what I was doing.' My colleague Willy Pajak told me that Dr Vasilevsky came from a great aristocratic family in Poland and was one of the best-known physicians there. He was a senior officer in the Polish army and a member of the resistance. He was also one of the people who formed the nucleus of the Polish resistance within the camp and had helped many prisoners, risking his own life in the process.

My mother suffered through the painful operation without uttering a sound. She herself does not remember how she managed to walk back to our block. *Blockälteste* Maria received her and put her in bed, where she passed out. She managed to stay in bed for a few days before she went back to work. Maria was constantly at her side.

How anxious I was, coming back from work every afternoon, to make sure that she would still be there. Even today she still has a deep pit behind her ear, which she covers with a long plait of hair.

Outside the camp, next to the PA offices, were the buildings where the SS lived, and a little further along stood the house belonging to the Camp Commander, Rudolf Höss. One day, it was a Sunday and very hot. I was sitting on a stone outside the building in the early afternoon. Suddenly I heard music coming from the SS buildings. The melody of the 'Spanish March' filled the air, and joy blossomed in my heart. Unbelievable! There was still music in the world! A small butterfly lost its way and flittered through the barbed wire, flying here and there. A butterfly here! I watched it, enchanted, and suddenly I realized that I had never seen a single flower or tree in the whole camp, not a single bird sang there. It was like a ray of light penetrating the camp's darkness. The sun was shining in the blue sky, there were butterflies, music could be heard.

My mother and I tried to locate the Greek women survivors of the transports and find out the *Kommandos* in which they worked. At every opportunity we would ask the messengers who commuted back and forth from one camp to the other. Many of them worked in the 'Shuh-Kommando', others in the 'Union-Metallwerke' and still others in Block 10.

Block 10 was located inside the men's camp in Auschwitz. A black wall joined it to Block 11. Block 11 was the '*Strafblock*' (punishment block), and in the basement were the bunkers. The bunkers were special cells one meter square in which prisoners could not lie down and had to stand or sit with their legs drawn up. What a torture it must have been not to be able to lie down when they were put in there with their bleeding and tortured bodies. Most of them could not hold out and died before they were removed. Very few survived.

All the prisoners to be punished had to first go through an 'interrogation' by the PA Department. 'Interrogation' meant torture, and one of the worst torturers was SS Staff-Sergeant Friedrich Wilhelm Boger. Many times in the evening my workmates Maryla Rosenthal and Aranka Pollak would talk to us about the 'interrogations'. They were themselves terribly shaken they told us, for the prisoners' screams of desperation and pain echoed in their ears incessantly, making sleep impossible.

I remember Maryla telling me, full of awe and horror, about the '*Boger Schaukel*' – Boger's swing. It was his own invention, which he himself called his '*Sprechmaschine*', a machine that makes people talk. It was a swing to which prisoners were tied by their hands and feet and tortured for one or two hours, sometimes longer. 'When they brought someone back on a stretcher,' according to Maryla, 'he no longer looked like a human being. He could not stand or walk. His face was often completely contorted.'

Despite the difference in our ages, a close friendship developed between Aranka Pollak and me. She had been brought to the camp from Czechoslovakia in the spring of 1942. Aranka had completed a specialized program of business studies. Fluent in German and trained in German shorthand, she had worked for a well-known German firm until her arrest. She treated me as if I were her daughter and often had something new to tell me about the happenings in her department. The papers of men arriving from the Paviak prison or other terrible Gestapo prisons in the different occupied countries often required their interrogation. This was SS-man Boger's job.

Once, when the day was especially 'torturing', as Aranka told me characteristically, she grabbed my arm and with tears in her eyes said: 'Listen my little one, listen carefully to all that we say to you and try never to forget anything you see and hear in this place. You might survive. I certainly will not, and then you must speak out and tell what happened here.' Fortunately, both Aranka and Maryla survived, and they have also told of their experiences in Lore Shelley's book.

The black wall that joined Blocks 10 and 11 was the wall where executions were held. Block 10 was the block where experiments were performed on prisoners by Dr Mengele (PhD and MD) and Professor Dr Clauberg. Women were housed in one wing, and we heard that the majority were Greek. The transports from Greece were arriving one after the other at that time (1943–44), and from these transports they would choose young girls, 'virgins' and young married women. Among others, they experimented in hopes of finding ways to sterilize men and women faster and more effectively. This was basically Dr Mengele's specialty. Dr Clauberg would bring as many twins from the transports as he wanted to the block. I don't know what his criteria were. They were known as 'Clauberg's twins'.

I tried many times to find out what happened there, but everything was concealed under an air of mystery and nobody 'knew' anything. We did not know how many Greek girls there were, nor did we know their names. People often spoke about the Greek girls who were supposedly there. Even after the liberation I could not find out very much. I met some girls who survived Block 10, and even some of the men. When I tried to ask them about various things that happened, they would only reply evasively. But at least I discovered that they had been experimented on without anesthetics. 'It was terrible, horrible,' and they did not want to talk about it. Their inner 'doors' had closed, so traumatic were their experiences there. I regarded them with awe and did not dare to ask any further questions.

The same thing happened to me in a way. When I returned from the camp I wanted to talk to people, to tell them what happened in the concentration camps, to make them understand the level of brutality and inhumanity to which people could sink when they let themselves be possessed by their worst instincts. The few times I tried to talk about my experiences, I realized that everything I had said was so horrifying that it seemed unbelievable that these terrible things could have happened. People wanted neither to listen to me nor to believe my story. They would look at me as if I were from a different planet, and I could read in their eyes: 'Stop, I think you are exaggerating, things like that don't happen!'

So, little by little, all the burning memories came to be hermetically locked away in the back of my mind. I had to live, to find myself, to start my own family. 'Leave things as they are, don't poison your life or that of the people around you, it will not change anything anyway,' I would tell myself.

Fifty years later, when together with Alberto Nar we interviewed the few remaining survivors, I opened the hermetically sealed compartments of my mind. I learned more details about what happened in Block 10, and I could not sleep for many nights. Still, what they said was little in comparison with the horrible reality they had lived through.

A few girls who had come from Greece with us worked in Birkenau's Schuh-Kommando. 'At least they have a roof over their heads,' I thought, 'protected from the cold.' Others worked in the 'Canada'-Kommando. This was a privileged *Kommando* where men and women worked separately. The men did the heavy jobs; they carried the luggage belonging to Jewish deportees that had to be left on the station platform. The possessions were typical of the places the prisoners came from. The workers had to sort clothes according to their style, putting the most expensive clothes into separate piles: coats, furs, leather items, each category arranged separately. The same with the handbags, shoes, hats, jewelry, paper money and gold coins. They had to check the hems, seams, soles of shoes and remove anything people had hidden there in their desperation.

'Canada' was the land of promise; it meant wealth. Whatever was of good quality or useful the SS sent back to Germany, they kept the shabbier things for the prisoners. After they sorted them out they painted a red line on the back of the items using oil paint. Prisoners who had an important position, like the *Kapos* or the people in charge of a block, could keep the nicest things for themselves. They painted the red lines very neatly or instead of oil paint they would often sew on a red ribbon.

The *Kapos* kitted themselves out with short blue overcoats from 'Canada', which they wore over their striped uniforms, and they would strut around the camp's streets, proud and very elegant in shiny black boots. They wore a wide yellow ribbon around their arms bearing the word *Kapo*.

The girls who worked in 'Canada' managed to smuggle clothes out by wearing two or three items under their camp uniforms. Of course it was a very risky business, and if they were caught the SS punishment was merciless.

I remember that one of the 'Canada' girls brought me a pink blouse to wear under my striped dress. It was such a luxury! I even let a bit of pink show above the neckline of my uniform. Naturally I considered myself very elegant. I wore that blouse constantly until we left Auschwitz.

Many Greek girls worked in the 'Union-Werke'-Kommando. It was a munitions factory, and demand was increasing. Production had to be expanded, and they needed more workers. The girls who already worked there recommended their 'sisters' and 'cousins', and in this way a few more girls managed to survive. Many men also worked in the Union-Kommando. The girls would often find a way to talk to them.

They always had some 'good news' to tell them: 'The war is lost for the Germans. Be brave, the Russians are coming soon. The Germans will not hold out much longer.'

But the war continued, and life went on in the camps with the same harsh cruelty. New transports continued to arrive from Germany, Yugoslavia, Poland, Belgium and France.

It must have been July or early August 1943 [19 July] when a colleague from the men's camp came into the offices of the Politische Abteilung. He was obviously very confused and whispered to our *Kapo*, Edith, that they had taken ten men from Block 11 and hanged them on ten gallows which they had set up in front of the camp kitchen. They had called all the men to line up for a roll call, forcing them to watch the execution as an example for anyone considering an escape attempt.

During that period transports were arriving continuously. Many of them were from Sosnowitz, and we registered each RSHA arrival: 'Ca. 3,000 people arrived, 110 men registered with such-and-such numbers, and 195 women registered with such-and-such numbers ...' We were all overwhelmed by a terrible feeling of depression. There were many transports, and the numbers of people sent to the gas chambers and the numbers 'admitted' to the camp didn't differ much from one transport to the next. Would the trains ever stop coming and unloading their human freight?

On one of these days, no SS-personnel happened to be in the office. One of our colleagues called my mother and me, '*Kommt! Schaut!*' (Come! Look!) We peered out the window at an endless line of trucks filled with prisoners heading for the gas chambers and crematoria. In one of the trucks we could see little children waving their hands. An unforgettable picture of the Sosnowitz transports was permanently printed in my mind.

What shocked me most was when they caught prisoners who had escaped. Every so often there was a report to the office that prisoner no. *x* had escaped. I had to take his file out of the cabinet and send it to the interrogation department. Good luck to the person who had managed to escape and a prayer for him not to be caught! And what a disappointment it was when the file came back with the notation *'Auf der flucht verhaftet'* (caught trying to escape). How much was concealed behind that sentence. The violent chase by the SS-men and their dogs, the prisoner's agony, his frantic efforts to find a hiding place, his desperation ... Usually it was the Poles who tried to escape. How could a French, Dutch or Greek prisoner think of escape without knowing a word of Polish?

Even the ones who tried to escape had difficulty with the local people. They could easily recognize them by their appearance, and there were many collaborators.

Every escape from the camp meant a new crisis. The SS-people became terribly tense and angry, as though they were personally offended. They took it out on the prisoners, keeping them standing at attention outside for hours during the *Appell* in cold weather or hot until they determined who was missing. They seized the prisoners who slept or worked with the escapees and interrogated them, always using torture. The escapees who were caught were placed in an area surrounded by barbed wire. A piece of white cloth with a black spot in the middle was sewn on the back of their uniform so that all the prisoners could recognize them.

The fugitives who were not shot during their capture and survived the bunker were put in the Strafkommando, the punishment detachment, where the living conditions and the work were even worse than hard labor. Most of them did not last long.

Despite living conditions better than those in the rest of the camp, our food was unpalatable, and we were constantly hungry. One of our Politische Abteilung colleagues from Vienna, Berta, used to say, 'When I get out of here the first thing I will do is to eat a schnitzel as big as a water closet cover!' Every time I cook a schnitzel I think of her.

The months went by, the cold winter came, and I got more used to the camp routine, trying to understand its little 'secrets'. I became very close friends with Reni, who worked in the laundry. Her job was to wash the SS-personnel's clothes.

Often, as we were returning from work, I would go to the laundry to look for her and to wash my clothes. After a while she would take them to wash herself. She was two years younger than I. She had lived with her family in Berlin, and she would talk to me about her life there. How different it had been from my life!

I also made friends with Jacqueline, a French girl. She worked in the tailor shop and often came over, or I went to her bed, to chat. She didn't speak any German, so we spoke French together. I spoke very little French, although a French tutor used to come to our house. I had considered the lessons a burdensome chore, just like my piano lessons. Now my French was helping me to communicate with Jacqueline, who constantly corrected me and helped me to improve. Jacqueline had five younger siblings, and when they arrived at Birkenau they were immediately sent to the gas chambers, together with her parents. She was often overwhelmed by despair and would cry in a heartrending way when she was depressed. She was a sweet, very intelligent girl with a great sense of humor.

Unfortunately I lost touch with her, despite efforts to locate her. After the liberation I immediately got in touch with Reni, though. I had repeated my address to her many times – it was an easy one in Thessaloniki, '15 Venizelos Street', which she always remembered despite everything she went through. As soon as she was released from the sanatorium where she recovered for six months, she wrote to me. Today she lives in Israel.

It is a strange fact that whenever we spoke with our fellow prisoners we all expressed our certainty that we would never leave the camp alive. The SS-people themselves constantly reminded us of this.

Once the director of the PA, SS-man Kirschner, was in a bad mood – more and more common as time went by – which made us all the more terrified of him. He told us: 'If you keep on behaving like this, it will be that much sooner that you will be sent to the gas chamber and be turned into smoke rising from the smokestacks.'

We all lived with a Damocles Sword hanging over our heads. However, despite the many trials I went through, I became convinced in the course of all those years that I would one day return to my beloved hometown and the friends who lived there. Consequently, whenever I thought of giving someone my address in Thessaloniki, without any hesitation I would say, '15 Venizelos Street', the address where my father's shop is still located today.

In the meantime we saw my father a few more times, standing in front of Block 1 and gazing in our direction. To this day I remember my heart beating from excitement and joy when I saw my brother standing there one day. So tall and so very thin! I wanted to call him, to talk to him, to hug him.

The holidays were passing by without our even being aware of them. But in a strange way, although we did not have a calendar, we always knew when it was Yom Kippur. Besides, the Germans did not let us forget it. The biggest selection was held on the day of Yom Kippur. The sorting out – '*Sortierung*', as the SS called it – started at the morning roll call. They went from block to block and took any prisoner who stayed behind or was wandering aimlessly around the camp. The same thing happened during the march of the outside *Kommandos* through the camp's gates, at the hospitals – *Krankenbau* and *Krankenhaus* – and again in the evening during the *Kommandos'* return from work. That day the selection was made with special cruelty. This happened in all three camps of men and women in Auschwitz and Birkenau. The typewriters in our office worked non-stop. We had to write the SB lists with all the names. There were over a thousand.

I would observe the Czechoslovakian and German women who lived together. Most of them were so religious. They believed in God above, and they would pray so fervently each day. They knew all the prayers by heart and always knew what day it was. I wondered what made them so religious? How could they believe in a God who accepted all the injustice, all the terrible crimes, the unthinkable misery? What were they praying for, I asked myself, as I saw the SS-people becoming more and more cruel. How could I believe that God is merciful? I felt so rebellious, having so many questions without answers.

The four new crematoria worked non-stop. Close to Christmas we heard of another big selection in the Birkenau women's camp. They 'selected' and burned more than 1,000 women one day. At almost the same time 2,500 persons arrived from Theresienstadt. After the selection the people temporarily permitted to live were brought to the 'family camp', a new section at Birkenau.

Fifty years later I read Danuta Czech's *Calendar of Events in the Concentration Camp Auschwitz-Birkenau 1939–1945* (published as *Kalendarium der Ereignisse im Konzentrationslager von Auschwitz-Birkenau 1939–1945*, Reinbek, 1989). It is a very thick book, listing in detail what happened in the camps on each day, starting with the day the camp was opened and ending with the last day in 1945. Every statement is supported, either by German official documents or other evidence. I am filled with awe and rage at the scale of the crimes the Germans systematically committed.

I wrote about 2,500 people who came from Theresienstadt, because that is what I remembered. But the reality is that every day, every week, thousands of Jews arrived and the gas chambers operated non-stop. Anyone who is interested can learn about this by reading Danuta Czech's book. It is especially relevant for anyone who thinks that the Holocaust never took place.

The year 1944 came without any change in our lives, without

any hope. But something was stirring in the outside world. One of my colleagues found a newspaper on the desk of an SS-man and secretly read it. Although the newspaper was German, the news about the German war effort was not good at all. We would talk about it in our beds at night, full of excitement, wondering if something decisive would happen soon.

5 • *Times of Terror and Hope of Survival*

The 26 March 1944 was a day like any other, but for me personally a very special day. It is the day on which I sensed what love, brotherhood, assistance and creativity there was in the camp despite all the torturers. For in this hell that they had created for us there was still a ray of sunshine.

It was my birthday, and my friends did not want the occasion to pass unnoticed. When we returned from work that evening, I found a small flower on my bed, around which several items had been arranged. I stood there, my mouth open wide with surprise, and a lump in my throat from emotion that left me speechless. Even today when I remember this occasion it brings tears to my eyes.

The girls were gathered around me in anticipation. 'Many happy returns,' my friend Reni wished me, and with a wink she added, 'Did you think we had forgotten your birthday?' From the bed she took a starched white kerchief for my head and gave it to me. Gisela gave me an onion with a red band tied in a bow around the end. Edith Vessely and her sister Renée had made a tiny cake from two portions of bread kneaded together with jam, and on top there were bits of margarine which looked like whipped cream. Maryla had taken the flower from the vase belonging to Staff-Sergeant Boger. And there was a pale blue nightgown with pink flowers from my mother. It had been smuggled in by the 'Canada'-Kommando, I have no idea how. What a surprise! My God, was it possible, I asked myself, that this was happening to me?

One day my mother and I were called to the office next door. A specialist in 'racial science' and his assistant had arrived

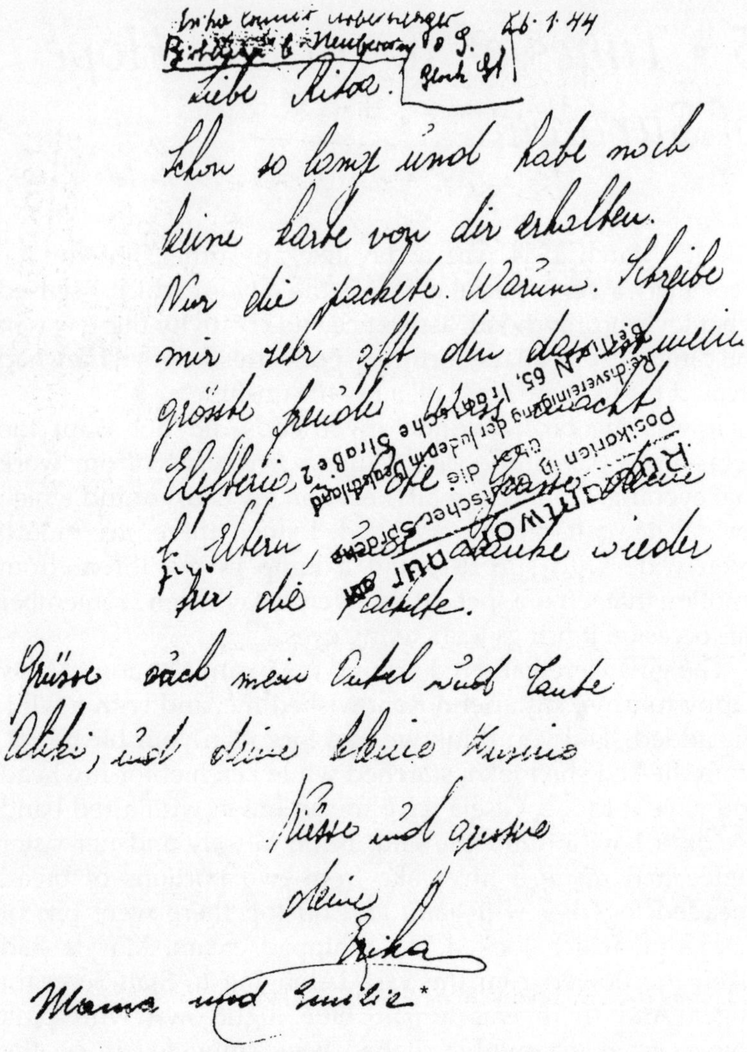

Liebe Ritsa:

Schon so lang und habe noch keine Karte von dir erhalten. Nur die Packete. Warum. Schreibe mir sehr oft den das ist meine grösste Freude. Was macht Elfteria, Pote. Grüsse deine l. Eltern, und danke wieder für die Packete.

Grüsse auch mein Onkel und Tante Alki, und deine kleine Kusine

Küsse und Grüsse

deine

Erika

Mama und Emilie*

Letter sent by Erika Kounio from Birkenau, 26 January 1944.

* Dear Ritsa, It is so long and I did not receive any card from you. Only the parcels, why? Write me often because, it is a big joy for me. How are Elefteria and POTE? Greetings to your dear parents and thank you again, for the parcel. (*Elefteria* means Freedom in Greek, *pote* means when.)

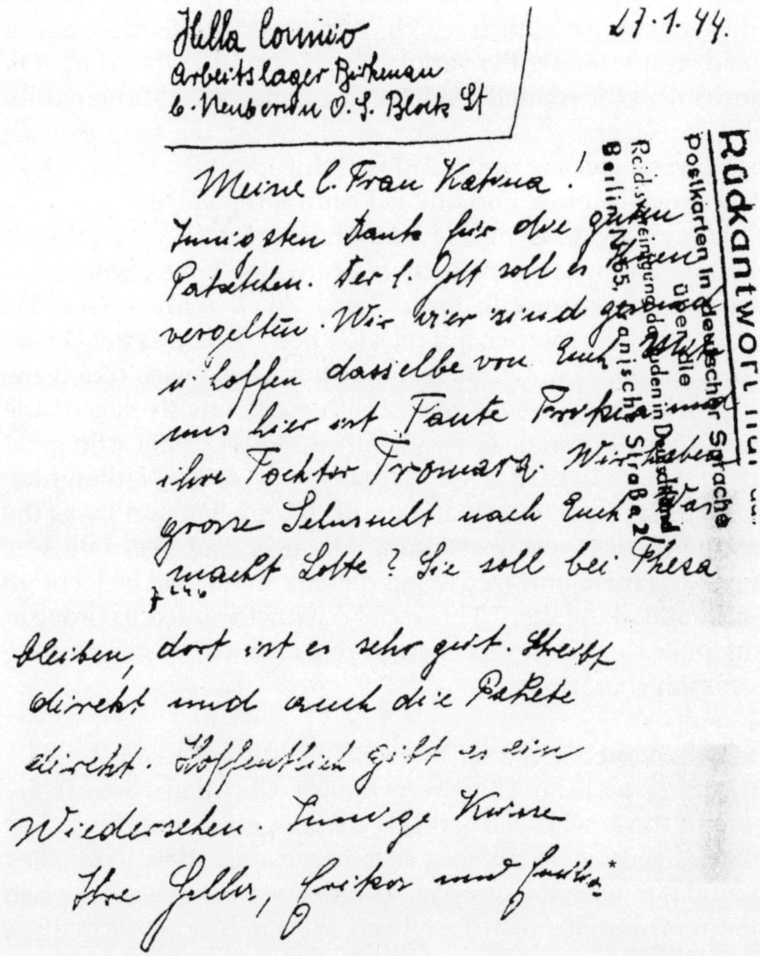

Hella Kounio
Arbeitslager Birkenau
b. Neuberun O.S. Block 24

27.1.44.

Rückantwort nur in deutscher Sprache
Postkarten in deutscher Sprache über die
Reichsvereinigung der Juden in Deutschland
Berlin N 65, Iranische Straße 2

Meine l. Frau Katina!
Innigsten Dank für die guten Paketchen. Der l. Gott soll es Ihnen vergelten. Wir vier sind gesund u. hoffen dasselbe von Euch. Mit uns hier ist Tante Frikia und ihre Tochter Tromara. Wir haben grosse Sehnsucht nach Euch. Was macht Lotte? Sie soll bei Thesa bleiben, dort ist es sehr gut. Schreibt direkt und auch die Pakete direkt. Hoffentlich gibt es ein Wiedersehen. Innige Küsse
Ihre Hella, Erika und Familie.*

Letter sent by Hella Kounio from Birkenau, 27 January 1944.

* My dear Mrs Katina I thank you dearly for the good parcels. May the dear Lord repay you. We all four are well and hope the same for you. Here with us are aunt Friki and her daughter Tromara. We miss you so much. How is Lotte? She must stay with Thesa it is very good there. Write to us directly, as well send the parcels directly. We hope that we will see you soon again. Many kisses, Your Hella, Erika, and family. (*Friki* means horror in Greek, *tromara* means fright).

from Berlin, and they had been allocated space to carry on their 'research'. This 'research' consisted in making casts of heads representing the various 'races' found in the camp. On one wall of the room there were some shelves, and there were already several plaster heads on them. At the base of each head was a piece of cardboard with the identification 'Gypsy', 'Ukrainian', 'Polish' and others I cannot remember.

Somebody from the SS had told the researcher that among the persons who worked there were two Greek women. It was an opportunity to make 'heads' of the Greek race. He questioned my mother, but rejected her, as she was not Greek. Then he called me in. It seemed that he likewise found me insufficiently representative of either the Jewish race or the Greek. He again called in my mother and asked her with great insistence whether I were really my father's daughter. Perhaps she had had an affair with a Christian and I was the result? He kept on questioning her over and over and was more and more annoyed at her denials. In the end he let us go without making casts. This racial scientist wanted to prove at any price that the Jews belonged to a race with distinguishing common characteristics.

As I mentioned at the start, several men also worked at the PA in our *Kommando*. They were Polish Christians, who were among those who had worked the longest in the camp. Just like us, they were all sure that because of their work they would not leave the camp alive. Our surprise was great when one morning, it must have been in March or April of 1944, they did not appear for work. They had been transferred to another *Kommando*, and we never saw them again in our offices. They were not killed, and after a few months I learned that they had even freed Feliks Mylyk. I had to locate his file and send it on.

From the messengers I heard that a small resistance group had formed at the very start in the men's camp. Polish political prisoners, because of their work, came into contact with free Polish workers employed in the camp. In this way they learned what was happening in the outside world. Many Polish prisoners wrote to their families, who lived nearby, sending messages and detailed reports of what was going on inside the camp. The free workers were paid with jewelry, golden coins and paper money found sewn into the clothes of victims by the 'Canada'-Kommando, and these were smuggled out at great personal danger by electricians, plumbers or carpenters, depending on the sort of repair the building needed. Of course it was strictly forbidden to speak to the prisoners working there, but they always found opportunities to speak and to take out things they had been given, in the form of money or jewelry.

All this involved great danger to their lives. Many times I had to find the folder of number 'so-and-so' and send it to the PA interrogation department. Most of them ended up in the bunkers of Block 11. From there they either sent them to the punishment block or executed them against the wall of Block 11.

The Poles bribed the SS to keep silent by giving them jewelry, fur coats and anything else they wanted. The items were sent to their families in Germany. This was of course illegal for the SS, and the penalty was severe. We learned all this from the messengers or prisoners, as occasionally they were assigned to the offices at Birkenau when there was a lot of work to do.

From the beginning there was a nucleus of resistance in the camp. At first it was rather limited and insignificant, but starting in mid-1944 and continuing thereafter it became quite important. The frequent escapes created serious annoyance and irritation for the SS, who were unable to prevent them. To weaken the resistance, a large transport of Poles, mostly Christians, was assembled. All had low numbers, which meant that they had served the longest in the camp. They were transported from Auschwitz to a camp in Germany. I learned about this from Maryla, and received more details from Aranka Pollak, who always, but always, told me everything.

Our contacts with the men's camp became less frequent and occurred only when a PA prisoner from the men's camp came for files. The war news got worse and worse for the Germans. This seemed to make them more aggressive. The number of transports from the various countries of Europe to the camp increased.

Eichmann came to the camp for an 'inspection' in early 1944 [29 February 1944]. What was happening? Why had he come? We were all terribly upset! One messenger who came from Birkenau filled with anxiety told us that between 80 and 100 prisoners had been ordered to reinforce the Sonderkommandos (special squads working in the gas chambers). What were they preparing for now?

Part of the men's camp was fenced off, segregating the gypsies and their families. They also had a number tattooed on their left arm. Before their number stood the letter 'Z' for '*Zigeuner*' (gypsy). Every time a child was born, he or she was also given a serial number, and the lists of the new-born babies were sent to our office for filing. The same applied to those who died. We had to separate their files from the 'section of the living' and transfer them to the basement, where the 'section of the dead' was located. The gypsies lived there for a number of months, but one day we learned that the gypsies' camp was being cleared out. They had all been sent to the gas chambers (2 August 1944).

In Czechoslovakia, outside Prague at Theresienstadt, there was a camp which the Germans called a *Familienlager*, or family camp. This camp was a showcase – *Vorführlager* – where the prisoners lived together with their families. Despite the fact that the living conditions were pathetic, with hunger and severe illnesses rampant there, the prisoners tried to maintain a certain standard of living. Unexpectedly, we started receiving inventories from the RSHA (German Security Department) with lists from Theresienstadt (Fall 1944). Nearly every day 2,500, 2,000 or 3,000 people arrived who, after the selection, were taken to a wing at Birkenau where they also kept the families together. I was curious to know what this meant, whether they had decided to liquidate Theresienstadt.

It must have been late May or early June 1944 when those of us who were still alive were transferred from the staff building – *Stabsgebäude* – to a new building, Block 6, inside the men's camp. It was fenced off with a double line of electrified barbed wire. Our 'sleeping rooms' – *Schlafräume* – were more comfortable and we also had a big hall, which was dominated by a large table in the center of the room. As we learned later, they also transferred the girls from Block 10 to the same building. We never had any contact with them, nor did we see any women. They were totally isolated from us, and we knew nothing about them except that Professor Dr Clauberg was responsible for this wing of the block. It was a great mystery.

In our new block a new group of girls was also housed. Among them was Vera, who came from Belgrade. She was a beautiful girl, brunette with beautiful green eyes. She was not Jewish and came from a prison where she had been incarcerated for many months. We immediately became close friends. Vera told me about her mother and two brothers and her beautiful Belgrade. She was three years older than I. For more than a year she had worked as a courier for the underground movement. In one of the German's *razzias* she was caught together with some others. Without thinking, she told me, she had seized the gun of the German who was leading her, walking in front, and shot him. Why hadn't they killed her immediately? My curiosity was so great that I searched for her file. I read exactly the story that Vera had told me, as well as many other details about her activities. My admiration for her increased.

She had a beautiful voice, and one evening she softly sang 'Evening Bells', an old Russian song. All conversation suddenly stopped in the room so that people could listen to Vera better. Maria, our *Blockälteste*, came over, emotionally aroused and fearful, wanting to stop her. Conversation and making any noise was strictly forbidden after 'lights out', but instead she stopped, enchanted, and stood listening until Vera had finished. Without our realizing it, SS-woman Volkenrath had entered silently and was also listening. From then on, Vera often sang various songs from her country for us, but always without exception she began with 'Evening Bells'. What happened to Vera? I have never learned what became of her. I often wonder whether she survived or perhaps perished in the end.

The 'transports' continued to arrive in the same numbers from France, Belgium and Yugoslavia. Almost every day we had new arrivals by the thousands. The number of those selected to enter the camp remained about the same with each transport, between 200 and at the most 500 men and women altogether. The rest were taken directly to the gas chambers.

Suddenly, without warning, transports started arriving from Hungary, one after the other (from the middle of May to early July 1944). Information was coming in steadily over the grapevine. Thousands, many thousands, arrived daily at the railroad platform of Birkenau. Many of the railroad cars were not immediately unloaded, and the prisoners had to wait endless hours for their turn to come. A great line of prisoners was created, leading directly from the station platform to the gas chambers, instead of having the victims driven through the camp in trucks. The crematoria worked non-stop, yet still they could not keep up. They dug deep pits, threw wood and corpses into them and set them on fire. They burned the dead there, because the crematoria could not cope with such a massive influx.

We were all greatly aroused, could not sleep at night, and a terrible despair overwhelmed us. My religious colleagues prayed at night before going to bed, and we all tried incessantly to find out what was happening around us.

Dounia, one of the PA messengers, told us one day when the SS were away from the office that endless lines of people were standing outside the station waiting their turn to die in the gas chambers and be burned in the crematoria. 'As I was coming here,' she continued, 'I saw women in their summer dresses, many holding a parasol to protect them from the sun, others holding their babies and children! They were waiting patiently – for what? …' This scene has remained burned into my memory all these years, as if I had watched it in person.

The smell of burnt flesh lingered in the air, and at night the heavens were glowing red – and this went on for weeks that seemed unending.

One time somebody brought news that the SS were throwing live infants and young children up to two years old into the flames in the fire pits they had constructed. We could not sleep at night in our anxiety and agony. What could we do? Would the trains ever stop coming we wondered?

'If we ever leave this place alive, I say to you again,' my dear friend Aranka told me, 'you must never forget this, and you must tell it, so the whole world will know what is happening here.' She repeated these words exactly as she had done before.

How could I ever forget all this horror, as much as I tried to erase it from my memory? The picture that I had in my mind has haunted me all these years.

Hundreds of thousands of people disappeared – without a trace.

A Polish colleague in the PA was assigned to work for the 'Canada'-Kommando. He was away for the entire day. The next day he was very upset and told me: 'You cannot imagine what is going on there. Piles of fur coats, winter coats, dresses, glasses, jewelry, gold coins, shoes, all in separate piles. They sort them after they have examined the seams, the stitching, the soles, the heels of the ladies' shoes to find anything that might have been hidden there and then send the items to Germany. Hundreds of baby carriages tied together in bunches of five have been sent to Germany.'

That summer, polka-dot dresses were in fashion – nearly

every woman had such a dress. So many were collected in 'Canada' that one of the SS-officers decided to give them to us. Our striped 'uniforms' were wearing out, and instead of the SS spending the money to get us new ones, they hit on this solution. Suddenly we were no longer garbed in the striped prison outfits, but were all dressed in blue dresses with large or small white polka dots.

Even today I can remember how beautiful I felt in a dress that covered my body so softly. What a luxury! I wondered what unfortunate person had worn this dress, where could she be now? 'Don't think! Harden your heart, just remember, remember what is happening in this place,' I told myself.

Throughout May, June and July of 1944 transports arrived daily from Hungary. The SS-people became extremely nervous and shouted constantly. Kirschner, the chief, was in a rage, and poor Edith Grünwald, his secretary, used to come out of his office white as a sheet to pass on his orders. Often their breath reeked strongly of Schnapps, and they worked in a semi-drunken state.

At the end of June some news threw our ranks into confusion. Mala Zimetbaum, our messenger, had escaped with a Pole named Edward Galinski. The beautiful Mala, my dear messenger, had escaped? How, with what, where? Questions unanswered. 'Don't think about it too much,' said Berta, 'only pray that they will not be captured.' The SS-people were furious. Mala had, in the course of time, won their trust, how could she dare to deceive them? Every morning upon our arrival at the office our first question was: 'Any news of Mala?' Great relief, no news. The same the next day and the day after.

Five or six days passed and Mala had not been caught. We started to hope. Mala had made it, besides she spoke Polish very well. Edward had prepared his connections with Katowice well. The tenth and eleventh days passed. We were sure they had made it, as they had not been caught up until now! What an important witness Mala will be, I thought. She had seen so much and knew precisely what was going on in the two extermination camps. She would have a lot to tell!

On the twelfth day the bubble burst. Mala and Edward had been captured. It was the first thing I learned when I arrived at the office that day. The SS were celebrating, and we were secretly crying inside. 'They brought her to the bunkers in Block 11,' Maryla, who worked in the interrogation department, told me. 'They are being tortured terribly; they want to find out the names of their accomplices.'

I couldn't bear to hear any more about Mala, the beautiful Mala (quick as a weasel), being tortured. How could she endure the torture, I wondered. I reflected that one of the interrogators would be Boger, inhumane Boger, the torturer of countless victims. Maryla told me that Mala did not utter a word, though, she did not betray anybody, and neither did Edward. We all talked about these two heroes with admiration.

They were transferred from Block 11 of Auschwitz to Birkenau, to the respective camp for men and women. They would be executed separately, and all the prisoners would have to attend their hanging.

One messenger told us the latest news: 'Mala is in Birkenau, and tomorrow she will be executed.' But Mala had other plans. During the time when one SS-man was reading her indictment she cut her veins. As soon as the SS-man realized this, he rushed to stop her, but with her hands full of blood she slapped him. She was transferred immediately to the hospital to stop her bleeding, but she died on the way. All of us spoke of Mala with admiration and pride.

Edward was hanged in the presence of all the prisoners. He himself kicked the stool from under his feet while singing the Polish national anthem. If the SS hanged him to frighten us and make an example of him, I think they achieved the opposite. We all felt only admiration and sympathy. For days we talked about Mala and Edward.

The transports continued. One transport from Poland

contained 2,500 people, but only 150 were registered. Of those who arrived 80 per cent were children. The 2,350 not selected to live were killed with gas. 'Try not to forget, remember the numbers,' I told myself, and for days before I fell asleep at night I repeated the things that I did not want to forget.

A new transport arrived from Theresienstadt with 2,500 people. The grapevine went to work. For the Germans the news was very bad. Rumors said that they had evacuated the camp at Lublin because the Russians were coming. Was this true? Was it possible?

Suddenly an order came from Oberscharführer (Staff-Sergeant) Kirschner: We are to collect all the files of those who had died up to now in the Auschwitz camp. They were loaded into a truck and, we learned later, were burned. 'What is happening,' we asked ourselves, They were covering their tracks.

'The IG Farben works have been bombed.' By whom? The Allies? Something was happening at last, a ray of hope was shining again.

'A transport has arrived from Greece,' a messenger told us. From where? How many? She couldn't tell us. Two days later the files arrived from the office at Birkenau for the people who were selected and admitted to the camp. They were all from Corfu and Athens (30 June 1944). We read and examined the Athens files, looking for the name of my father's brother, Vital. No, the name Vital Kounio was not in the Athens file. Great relief. 'Unless he did not enter the camp, but was sent straight to the gas chamber,' said mother. A black cloud of depression took possession of us.

What is a human being?, I asked myself. Every day, from all over Europe, the transports arrived, and every day hundreds, thousands of people were executed, and I thought I could not have felt greater sorrow, greater anguish. But when our own people arrived from Greece I suffocated, ready to burst with grief.

'The Commander of the camp is expecting a visitor,' Erwin,

a Polish political prisoner who worked at the PA in the men's camp, told us. We were unable to learn anything more.

Upon returning to our block from work in the afternoon, the same as every day, we understood! Maria, our *Blockälteste*, met us in a state of great excitement, her eyes shining. The sleeping rooms were especially tidy today. Before leaving we always made our beds, and the blankets had to be neatly folded, but today something was different. Curtains covered the two windows – we could not believe our eyes. Curtains! In the hall a carpet had been placed on the floor, and in the middle of the big table there was a great bowl full of flowers. We stared with eyes open wide, for we could not believe what was unfolding before our eyes. Flowers, carpet ... unbelievable. Maria explained that the camp commander had arrived for an 'inspection' at mid-day with a stranger dressed in civilian clothes. Later Maria learned that the stranger was a Red Cross inspector from Switzerland (29 September 1944). Naturally the following day the carpet, curtains and flowers were all taken away.

It appears that this visit bore good fruit, for one special morning postcards were distributed to us. We were told that we would be allowed to write to our people, whatever we wanted. There were restrictions on what we were allowed to write, and of course we had to say, 'that we were being treated well.' To write ... to whom ... Where? As though we could remember any addresses.

My mother had a cousin who lived in Geneva and worked for the International Red Cross. Let's write to him at the International Red Cross and see what happens. I remembered the address of my dearest friend, Ritsa Mamouna, now Gombou, in Athens. My mother wrote to Ritsa's mother, Mrs Katina, and also to my father's brother, who lived in Athens with his Christian wife. Perhaps they were still in Athens; his shop was located at 15 Stadiou Street.

We took a few more postcards, we were allowed to do this, so as to write in peace that evening in our block. What could we write in order to convey the 'message', to let them know what was happening? Of course it had to be written in German, and the postcards would be censored. My mother wrote to Uncle Vital, her cousin in Switzerland, and to Mrs Katina: 'We are all well, and "so and so" and their families (they were all relatives who had been executed or had died in the camp) are well and they are with 'Theresa' (my grandmother, who had died before our deportation from Greece)'. I wrote to Ritsa that my Aunt '*Fricki*' (Horror) and Aunt '*Tromara*' (Terror) were with us, along with my Cousin '*Pina*' (Hunger), but that we were eagerly awaiting my Cousin '*Eleftheria*' (Freedom) – using Greek words as though they were last names.

Suddenly a door to the outside world opened in my head. I began thinking constantly of all those I had left behind; how much I missed them and how much I had to tell them. I thought of various ways to express what I wanted to tell them to help them understand better, as though they could have done anything to free us.

For days I spoke to Ritsa in my mind, and in my mind's eye I continually saw our house near the sea, my lovely neighborhood, Mitso's Patisserie and Ivi making the best ice cream in the world, and gazing at the beautiful sunsets from the balcony of our house. There was an excruciating pain in my heart which had to be stilled. Here where I found myself there were other values, other things to occupy my mind. 'Close the door to yesterday, don't think! ... Look, listen, you must survive! ... Don't forget anything that you see here,' I told myself.

My cousin Fritz Ullman and Ritsa Mamouna did in fact receive their postcards and kept them. They gave them back to us upon our return from the camp, and some of them I gave to the Jewish museum of Athens, but the remainder I kept at home.

After a few weeks we received two small parcels containing raisins and dried fruit from my friend Ritsa in Greece and, three or four times, cans of Portugese sardines from my Uncle Fritz in Switzerland. These were the items that could be sent from their countries. After that all was silent; we received no more parcels. We learned that the Germans had made these 'good-will gestures' a few times and gave us the parcels, but thereafter they confiscated the parcels for their own use.

What excitement I felt when I received the first parcel from Greece. Ritsa was thinking of me and remembered me! I saw her before me and spoke to her. A feeling of tenderness filled my heart for my old friend. I spoke about Ritsa to my friends Reni and Jacqueline, and I felt as though we had never been separated. We were not allowed to write again.

A number of weeks had gone by since the last 'transport' from Greece. I thought that after the arrival of the Jews from Corfu and Athens there were no more Jews left in Greece. What a surprise when, in the inventory of new arrivals at Birkenau that we were given to enter and file, there was another list from Greece … This time from Rhodes. Together with mother, I looked over the inventory. The name Kounio appeared far more often than any other name. 'Are there so many Kounios?' I asked. 'Are they our relatives?' We could not imagine that we had so many namesakes on the island of Rhodes. I could not imagine that there were so many Jews on Rhodes. I wanted to meet the girls that arrived from there and learn about the name Kounio. Where did it come from? But that proved to be impossible. They were not brought to Auschwitz, but rather to Birkenau. I realized that from their numbers. The numbers given to the men had the letter B in front, and those of the women the letter A. These were the new numbers assigned, I believe from 1943 or early 1944 on, I assume because the first series of numbers, which included our own, was getting too long.

It was a beautiful day in September when we heard the alarm siren wail for a long time. This was the first time this had happened for us, and we were at a loss. Not only we, but also the SS. 'Go down to the basement quickly … You are forbidden to go out … Assemble …' We could hear the SS giving orders, running about like madmen, shouting. We had just got into the basement when we heard bombs exploding, and the whole building shook. My mother was in one part of the basement, and I in another. I was frightened, not being with her, and I started to look for her. Suddenly there was a frightening noise, and windows shattered. The girls screamed and threw open the doors. We all ran outside, without understanding what was happening. 'A bomb fell on our building! It is the English, they will free us,' we cried, still frightened.

I don't know how, but in the panic we found ourselves in the men's camp, and the men and women prisoners were standing together. Suddenly, without realizing this at first, I saw my father supported by my brother to keep him from collapsing. My father's face was covered with blood, and he was walking with his hands outstretched in front of him, unable to see. I embraced him and he held me tight in his arms, crying. I talked to my brother, after also embracing him. He told me that father had been hit by a piece of shrapnel. 'Luckily he is talking, luckily he is walking,' I thought.

This did not last for long. The totally shocked SS-people, who had scattered to seek shelter, started to get a grip on themselves: shouting, beating and threatening us with their guns, they separated us in order to drive us back to our barracks. Despite our anxiety, we were filled with joy, because we felt that something was soon going to happen, and that we would be free!!!

I had been standing next to a boiler in the basement at the start of the air raid, together with my friend Edith Winter. Not seeing my mother, I had gone to look for her, in order to be near her. Exactly at the spot where I had been standing the greatest damage took place. Edith was apparently struck by a bomb there and died instantly. Here again was another coincidence that saved my life!

For days I could feel my father's embrace. My brother's image was constantly in my mind. He had lost the childish appearance I remembered. In the one-and-a-half years that we had been separated he had grown so much. Luckily my father's injuries were not serious, and after two weeks we learned that he was doing well.

The transports kept on coming. Inventories with the names of those 'entering' arrived daily from the office at Birkenau. From Slovenia, from the Lodz ghetto. But how many had they managed to herd into this ghetto?

The 'Union-Werke'-Kommando was the largest 'female' *Kommando*. 'There must be more than 1,000 women working there,' we were told by our messenger, Dounia. At that time they created a small camp for women in Auschwitz I. They took seven buildings from the men's camp and surrounded them with double lines of electrified barbed wire. In this newly formed women's camp stood our Block 6. In the newly formed blocks now lived girls who worked in the Union together with the Jehovah's Witnesses who worked as servants in the houses of the SS-people, in the various sections of the PA and in other service areas.

In the women's camp at 'Auschwitz II' – Birkenau they held another big selection. More than 1,000 women were sent to die in the gas chambers. Who told us not to despair, that all this would soon come to an end? After a few days we learned that another 2,000 people had been murdered during a cleansing of the men's camp. We received no inventory with the 'SB' stamp, however.

From the Birkenau offices a strange list arrived to be entered which included about 200 men's names. At the top of this list we read '*Überstellt*' (moved) to another camp. At the end of the list there was an 'SB' stamp, i.e., special treatment. Something is not quite right, a colleague told me anxiously. From the letters SDK (Sonderkommando) we recognized that it had to do with prisoners who worked in the crematoria. We were all scared. They had started to liquidate the 'witnesses'!

After 50 years, the things I remember and write about are only a drop in the ocean. I read Danuta Czech's book *Calendar of Auschwitz* carefully so that I could cross-reference the events I have described and check whether I remembered them correctly. Again I became outraged and could not believe that these things took place daily. What a perfect machine of extermination the SS constructed! How could human beings in cold blood set up and operate such an efficient killing machine to murder so many millions of people?

The grapevine was celebrating victory! People talked about some form of 'invasion' by the Allies. 'Courage, girls!' Erwin told us, 'soon our torture will be over.'

One morning, arriving at the office, we found the SS in great turmoil. Angrily they accosted us, shouting constantly and continually walking from one office to the next. We did not know what was going on and were all cautious, trying to decide what was happening, what had happened … SS-Oberscharführer (Staff-Sergeant) Kirschner, the top boss, roared into the telephone. Her face pale, Edith Grünwald, his secretary, emerged from his office now and then to collect various inventories and various files. Only towards lunch-time did we learn what the commotion was about. They had blown up Crematorium IV. What? Who? 'The prisoners of the Sonderkommando!'

The Sonderkommando had mutinied? Had they rebelled? Was this possible; how did they do it? Who helped them? What happened, how many were killed? Thousands of questions which for the time being remained unanswered.

We continued our work. The typewriters worked continuously! I searched for the files the SS demanded from their office. That day – as so often – we did not return to our camp at the regular time in the afternoon, but stayed on late into the evening. Again Erwin, who came from the men's camp, gave us more information. One team of the Sonderkommando, together with the 'resistance' group of prisoners, had been planning this explosion for some time.

'But where did they get the explosives?' we asked. 'From the Union! – The girls who worked there have been smuggling explosives to the men for weeks!' Turning to me he added, 'The Greeks were in the front line of this uprising!' The Greeks, our own people, had raised their heads and stood up to them? I couldn't believe it. But it was true! I felt so proud of them. 'Definitely they will not escape,' I thought, 'but what a noble death! They will not be burned like the two hundred. They have chosen death in the way they wanted!' We continued to talk about this with my mother until late in the evening.

In the interrogation department at the PA there was now a great amount of work. Every day they brought prisoners from Birkenau whom they were suspicious of. The torture that accompanied the interrogations was terrible, and the girls who worked there were beside themselves. Maryla talked to me about it and cried the whole time. She could not stop hearing the screams and groans of the prisoners being interrogated. After interrogation all of them were taken to the bunkers in Block 11.

Together with the men they interrogated four girls from the 'Union'. The torture they were put through was frightening, we did not know where they were taken afterward. The interrogation lasted a number of days. Crematorium IV was not put back into operation again. We learned that some SS-people had been killed, but received no detailed information.

Every now and then we typed new lists with the names and numbers of the men and women (listed separately) who were transferred either to the gas chamber or to other camps in Germany. One big transport arrived in Birkenau from Ravensbrück, Germany. None of the prisoners were admitted to the camp; they were all *Muselleute* (walking dead) and were sent straight to the gas chambers, the messenger from Birkenau told us. Something was happening, but we could not tell what. There was much coming and going, and the crematoria worked non-stop.

At Birkenau there had for some time been a transit camp (*Durchgangslager*), where they housed prisoners who were to be sent to other camps. But one day we learned that this was not exactly the case. Thousands of people were jammed together without being accepted anywhere, as was the normal procedure according to the RSHA inventories of the PA. In this way the number of admissions to Auschwitz would not seem so large! The living conditions there were shocking; they were all just waiting for their turn to die. As soon as the gas chambers and the crematoria had a bit of extra capacity free, selections were made and 1,000, 2,000 or 2,500 people were killed at a time.

One morning we learned that the gypsy camp had been totally liquidated (10 October 1944). They gassed and burned 800 people in all.

Again we started to receive transports from Theresienstadt. 'But didn't they send them all the last time?' I asked myself. One thing followed another, we worked in a state of tension, and I tried to find out as much as I could.

One day (12 October 1994) my colleague Willy Pajak from the Auschwitz office came and whispered to me, 'Greece is free! The Germans have left.' This news struck me like a bolt of lightning. Unbelievable, Greece is free! So our liberation could not be long in coming. I do not know how I kept myself from embracing and kissing him. At the first opportunity I hastened to tell my mother. What emotion, I wanted so much to learn more details. But Greece was so very far away …

Life went on in the camp … Every now and again we heard planes flying overhead, but nothing happened. Time went by, and it was already late November 1944. A new list arrived with the names of men who had worked in the Sonderkommando: all had been executed. The number of survivors grew smaller and smaller.

The SS destroyed Crematorium III and attempted to

eradicate every trace. We wondered when our turn would come. This fear haunted us steadily.

December 1944 arrived and Christmas approached. The SS looked sullen and drank constantly.

It couldn't be very far off, the day of our liberation. From the 'free' Polish workers in the camp we learned the latest news. 'The Germans have lost the war!'

Increasingly more branch camps were evacuated, and the still-healthy prisoners in the camp were transferred to camps in Germany. The girls of our *Kommando* were continually busy preparing the lists of transfers. In the men's camp gallows were set up again. They hanged five prisoners in front of everyone at the *Appell*: 'setting an example' to intimidate those remaining.

So December came to an end and 1945 began.

It was 6 January 1945, a date I will never forget. At the evening roll call, which lasted a long time, all the women of the camp had to witness the hanging of four girls who worked in the 'Union'. Three of them had worked in the storehouse where the explosives and ammunition were kept. Secretly they had smuggled explosive materials to the men of the Sonderkommando. The Camp Commander screamed out the charges and ended with the words: 'This is how we punish all traitors.' They were Ella (Gärtner, Gartner), Roza (Roia, Robota), Regina (Safirstein, Saphierstein) and Esther (Estera, Wajsblum, Wajcblum).

We constantly heard the thunder of cannons and rumors on the grapevine that the Russians were approaching and would soon free us. But why didn't the Russians hurry if they were so near we asked ourselves.

Every day hundreds died, and the Germans continued their executions as though the Russians were not already at the gate.

One day, it must have been 10 or 12 January 1945, although the rumors were that the Russians had already reached

Katowice, the town closest to Auschwitz, our *Kommando* received the order: 'Drop whatever you are doing and proceed to the crematorium.' The crematorium referred to was an old one which was no longer in use. It had already been out of use in March 1943, when we arrived in the camp.

A few SS-men escorted us, and one of them carried a bunch of keys. They led us out. Five minutes later we found ourselves in front of a large 'gothic' gate which reminded me of the entrance to a castle. One of the SS-men tried to open the door with different keys. When the door opened, a sweet sickly smell forced its way into our nostrils. Holding our noses we entered.

Soon we found out where the smell was coming from. Decomposed corpses lay everywhere around us. We proceeded onward, passed through by an old gas chamber and entered another room where there were two huge ovens – a crematorium. An empty truck, on which corpses were piled and driven to the crematorium, was still standing there. All around us were skulls and bones and filth and a pervasive foul smell.

I was sure that they would execute us here, that our last moments had arrived.

When after a while the right key was found, an SS-man opened a door, and we found ourselves in a room with many rows of wooden shelves. Arranged in an orderly manner on the shelves, one next to the other, were big urns. We found ourselves in a huge ossuary, and our job was to 'clean' it.

An SS-man stood on a ladder and gave the urns one by one to the girls standing below, who passed them on from hand to hand. We formed a human chain leading to the entrance door of the crematorium, where the last girl gave the urns to the SS-men outside, who loaded them on to a waiting truck.

The urns were heavy, and as we were lifting them we could hear the rattling noise made by the bones. Our blackened hands hurt, but we continued our task, taking the urns and passing them on without stopping. For an instant I lost my grip on an urn, it slipped from my hand and fell to the ground … Ashes and bones covered me from head to feet. I thought I was going to faint, and the SS-man above me shouted: '*Schneller, noch schneller!*' (Faster, still faster!) Now and then we heard a crash as another urn fell, followed by hysterical laughter from one of the girls. We could not keep up this pace, our arms hurt more and more. The trucks were finally filled and drove off. Where they were headed we did not know.

For three whole days we worked continuously without stopping. One small break to eat, nothing would stay down, and then back to work again. How did we hold out? A girl asked an SS-man, 'The work left in the office – when will we do it?' The SS-man answered, 'That is not important, the most important thing is to clean the crematorium, and as fast as possible!'

There must have been thousands of urns. One girl mentions 6,000 in her testimony. These urns obviously belonged to Christian prisoners who had died since the camp was set up: of hunger, hardship and torture – not in the gas chambers.

For each urn they sent to the family of the prisoner a 'certificate' stating the cause of death: Heart attack, malaria and other various causes which I do not remember. The letter accompanying the death-certificate, which was sent to the family, was the same for all and said: 'Should you wish us to send you the urn with the ashes, remit [so many] German Marks.' It appears the families were not always interested.

After a few days in the office, another collection. The SS, with our help, stuffed documents, folders, lists and files on the prisoners into cardboard boxes and loaded them on to trucks. And the cannons could be heard coming closer and closer.

6 • *Ravensbrück, Malchov and Liberation*

It was 18 January 1945 – an unforgettable day. Chaos reigned in the camp. Trucks came and went, the SS were screaming out orders. From Birkenau women prisoners were being brought to Auschwitz, and the SS gave each prisoner a loaf of bread, a piece of margarine and a blanket. They formed columns of five, and endless rows departed through the camp gates, above which one could read the motto *'Arbeit Macht Frei'* (work makes you free).

We watched, not knowing what to do. Suddenly we heard an order: 'Politische Abteilung, present yourselves.' This is it, I thought, this is our end. A Polish prisoner, one of our co-workers, came to us and said: 'Go out quickly, join the others at once. Don't go anywhere, line up,' and then he left.

My mother grabbed my hand, and we joined the line to receive our bread and blankets. In the line we met three girls from Greece: Esterina, Sarah and Florika. We stood in a row together with the others, following the columns. I was haunted by the fear that SS-people would come and take us away …

It must have been noon when we set off, accompanied by armed SS-men. An SS-man marched next to every third or fourth row. It was bitterly cold, the roads were frozen, and the snow on the slopes was 30–40 cm deep. I thought of my father, and wondered whether he would be able to walk on the icy roads. Would he make it?

Before we set off, a higher-ranking SS-officer gave us our final instructions. I don't remember what he said, and I didn't understand everything. What I remember is that we had to walk fast, to keep our lines parallel, because any woman prisoner who could not keep up and fell behind would be shot on the spot.

For the last time we passed through the gate of Auschwitz and found ourselves on the road. Faster! Faster! the SS were yelling.

My mother constantly repeated … 'Go on, don't fall behind … Stay close together, don't stop … Don't look to the left or right, just look straight ahead …'

How could I not look to the left and right when the sides of the road were littered with corpses in striped camp uniforms. They were the first victims from the men's column that preceded us in the march. The farther we marched, the more corpses there were. I looked and thought: 'This must be father …,' and my mother shouted: 'Keep on, don't look, keep walking …'

For the first few miles we kept up with the pace. Our ears, noses and hands were frozen. It seemed like my blanket got heavier with each step, but we walked on and on.

'My legs won't last any longer,' cried Florika, and my mother held on to her, urging us on, 'Go on, don't fall behind, go on …'

These were the words I remember her repeating over and over, hammering them into my mind.

Every so often we heard gunfire and automatically accelerated our pace. The gunfire was meant for those who could not walk fast enough and fell behind, the last in the line. The more time passed, the more often we heard the sharp crack of gunshots.

The road was deserted, there were no cars, no people to be seen. Here and there far off in the distance stood a lone farmhouse. I don't remember that we made any rest stops anywhere, but when it became pitch dark we finally stopped in a big barnyard. One pressed against the other, we lay down on the straw and ate some dry bread. Florika cried in agony, her feet hurt so much.

Our shoes were now wet from snow, and our feet totally frozen. 'Don't take your shoes off,' my mother said prudently, 'they will freeze and you will not be able to put them on in the morning.' How right she was! Some of the girls took their shoes off and were unable to get them back on in the morning.

As we lay there on the straw, I asked myself whether I could hide there, buried in the straw, so I wouldn't have to join the column in the morning. I whispered my idea to my mother. 'Don't be foolish,' she told me, 'What would you do then? You don't speak Polish, they will immediately recognize you from the striped clothes you are wearing, they will kill you. Now we have to hold on; we are not far from the end.'

Throughout the night we could hear the cannons firing without a break and rockets falling, lighting up the darkness. 'Do you think the Russians will overtake us?'

We were so tired that we soon fell asleep, despite the cold and our hunger.

In the early dawn the next day the SS woke us with wild cries. Again we formed columns of five. The columns started off again. An interminable line of women walked on. Again on our left and right there were the fallen dead – and soon the shooting started all over again.

Now the road was less deserted, here and there a villager with his cart would pass by staring straight ahead. There were more houses; we marched through a village. 'This is Plasov,' (a village on the road to Vodzislav (Loslau) I heard a Polish woman say behind us. And my mother repeating constantly: 'Go on … Don't stop … Don't look around …' I couldn't help looking at the fallen bodies, and I was sure that 'this one' was definitely my father.

We stopped again in the evening in front of a large building. There was a large hall where we were crammed in, one against the other. This time there was no straw, and the cement floor we lay on was frozen. Florika was crying, it hurt so much. But how could we help her? The SS were chilled too, but, guns in their hands, they were ready to shoot anyone who fell behind.

I remember that I went out for some fresh air, and a Polish man passed by carrying a jug. We were extremely thirsty, and my mother was in a wretched state. I asked him if he could give me some water for my 'old' mother. I didn't say 'old' to impress him, I really did believe that my mother was old. She was thirty-nine. Only when I myself reached thirty-nine, only then did I realize how young my mother was during the camp years, and how old I thought she was.

The third day of the march dawned. We all hurt all over, but especially our feet. We had blisters, but who would give them a second thought. We walked and walked ... Florika became delirious. 'I can't walk anymore,' she told us. 'I will stay here.'

With an angry voice my mother grabbed her by the shoulders. Esterina and Sarah held her arms and dragged her along. We heard shooting from the back lines more and more often – and there were more and more corpses to the left and right! Another horrible night passed.

The fourth day and our column was getting smaller. We did not have anything warm to eat or drink all those days. The bread we had taken with us was gone; we were so hungry and thirsty!

The cannons didn't sound so close anymore, but many airplanes flew overhead.

Suddenly we arrived in front of a railway station. An endless line of open boxcars and a squad of armed SS-men met us. Our lips were swollen from all the snow we had eaten, and our thirst was becoming more and more unbearable.

We had reached the Loslau station, and with curses and wild screams they made us climb into the train. How many were in each wagon, 60, 70, 80? I don't know. In each wagon there were two SS-guards to watch us. We sat there exhausted. At least we don't have to walk anymore, I thought to myself.

The train set off. It was snowing and soon we, as well as the SS-people, were covered by a bright white blanket. We didn't have to walk anymore, but were almost as stiff as pillars of ice. How cold! My God, what frost! Clickety-clack, clickety-clack for endless hours. We went through several villages and one town and eventually the train stopped. How many days were we on the train? Two or three, I do not remember. I only know that our only nourishment was snow.

'Everybody out!' the SS-people shouted. Around us there was barbed wire, SS-men and women with dogs on leashes. We could hardly get off the train our arms and legs were frozen stiff and wouldn't move.

We were in the largest women's camp in Germany – Ravensbrück. They put us all into a huge hall that had belonged to Siemens (a major German manufacturing company). A picture of that first night is indelibly imprinted on my mind. An endless dark hall illuminated here and there by weak lights, and thousands of women squatting, pressed tightly against each other, groaning in delirium, swaying rhythmically as in lamentation.

I wanted to make a little space so that my mother could lie down, so I stood up. I immediately lost my place as a girl, also ill, stretched out her legs.

Like all the rest, my mother was extremely thirsty. Without thinking about what I was doing, I stood up and started towards the exit. It seemed to me to be a very long trip as I clambered over the seated women, accidentally stepping on hands or feet. I don't know why I did it, but I continued groping in the darkness.

Eventually I arrived at the door, which the SS had left wide open to ventilate the room. There was only one guard there, and he wouldn't let me out at first. I asked him to let me go out for a while. 'Don't worry,' I said, 'I don't intend to escape.'

I went out and sat on a ledge near the door. The freezing air invigorated me. As I looked around me, I noticed an empty tin can and picked it up. I could fill it up with snow and bring it back to my mother, who was so thirsty, I thought to myself. I asked the guard's permission to go a little bit further, where the snow was clean, and – amazingly – he didn't refuse. I ate some snow to quench my thirst, then I pressed as much snow I as could into the can and started to return.

What a hell! My God, I thought as I climbed over some sleeping women. Some of them, who were not asleep and saw what I was carrying, stretched their hands out to take away my snow. And hands raised high, I clutched the tin can so they would not take it from me. But it was a long and endless trip. By the time I reached my mother I was no longer holding anything. Two cunning hands had reached out deftly and snatched the can away with a cry. Eventually I found my way back to my mother, empty-handed and heart-broken. I burst into sobs.

The next morning two camp prisoners came in, each carrying a kettle of hot 'coffee'. I still wonder how these girls managed the distribution. Women were throwing themselves at them in order to get something warm to drink. Suddenly we heard gunshots. Frightened, we all became silent. Two of the SS-women had fired their revolvers into the air to re-establish order.

From the prisoners who carried the 'coffee' we learned that we were indeed in Ravensbrück, in the '*Jugendlager*' (concentration camp for youth), which they also called a '*Straflager*' (punishment camp). It was close to the central women's camp. Very young women were kept in huts hidden behind large, beautiful trees. Various different experiments were performed on them, though the girls could not tell exactly what they were. When we went out later, I saw a scene which has stayed in my mind permanently in every detail until today.

It was a very gray day, frozen, and the fog obscured the surroundings. Mud from the melting snow covered the ground, and only on the side were there piles of snow. In the distance we could vaguely make out huts located among tall trees. Every now and then two or three women could be glimpsed walking in the distance. They looked as if they had come from a different planet, for they were seemingly gliding along on rollers. Gray figures who didn't look to the left or right but only straight ahead. As in a dream I watched them disappearing into the woods. I wondered what had been done to them, what they had gone through to make them so apathetic.

Suddenly five girls passed me accompanied by an SS-woman. They were not wearing striped clothing, but rather black or gray dresses, and they were not walking but rather hopping along like rabbits. I asked one of the camp prisoners who those girls were, and she quickly told me that they were from the 'Experimentation Block'. 'Oh! The poor girls, the poor girls,' I screamed and sobbed inwardly. In the 'Youth Camp' at Ravensbrück they also had many pairs of twins the SS had obtained for the Experimentation Block.

We stayed in the camp for two or three weeks. The worst that I can remember. After that they divided us up into different groups and transported us to smaller annex camps affiliated with Ravensbrück.

The five of us, together with many other women, were taken to Malchov, a small women's camp, where they apparently used women prisoners to work in many small cottage industries.

It was a beautiful spot with many trees all around. Things were different there. It was not an extermination camp like Auschwitz, but a labor camp. The male guards were not SS-men, they belonged instead to the German army, the 'Wehrmacht'. They were older men. They seemed very tired and never yelled. Only their guns were ever-ready in their hands. There were few SS-men, but many SS-women.

We were finally given warm soup to eat after so many days, and in the evenings they gave us bread with margarine and a teaspoon of jam and sometimes even cheese, though it had an unpleasant musty odor.

They put me in a *Kommando* with 20 girls who worked together away from the camp in a box factory. The work was not hard, and the environment was pleasant. We had to make grooves in pre-cut pieces of cardboard so they could be folded into cardboard boxes.

I felt as if I were in paradise! Every morning we set off for the box factory accompanied by two Germans. We had soup for lunch and came back in the evening.

My mother stayed in the camp and worked in the 'Garden Kommando'.

I do not remember where the other girls worked, but the three Greek girls lived with us in the same barrack. My mother was the 'mother of the detachment', and together with the three girls we formed a little 'family'.

I worked there until approximately the middle of March 1945.

Now and then the snow and rain would stop and a weak sun would come out. It was as if the sun were warming up my heart, this life-giving sun in the always-gray, never-blue sky of Germany.

Life in this camp was so different from that in Auschwitz. Even the SS-guards were not as vicious, let alone the regular German guards. They knew for certain that the war would end with their defeat. We did not hear much news about the course of the war, because we were so isolated, but we could feel it 'in the air'.

Our biggest longing was for my father and brother. Thinking rationally, I concluded that my father could not have survived the death march, but deep inside me I still believed that he was alive. I talked about them daily with my mother, and we felt a constant pain and concern for them.

One day they took me from the box factory together with two other girls and put us in a different *Kommando*. We were to work in an SS kitchen three kilometers away from the camp. Our job was to peel vegetables, potatoes, small cabbages, big radishes, carrots, celery – good for soup.

Here we were definitely in paradise! While peeling we surreptitiously ate carrots and cabbages. Apart from that they gave us good soup, and we could ask for a second helping.

My mother continued working in the camp garden, where she got very little to eat.

'We have to get organized,' said the bravest of us, and of course we all followed her example. We all wore the striped dresses, underneath a long shirt and long breeches made from striped fabric – blue-and-white stripes – with elastic bands that tightened around our legs just over our knees, an apron over the dress and a kerchief on our heads. Since leaving Auschwitz nobody had cut our hair, and we were pleased that it was starting to grow out again. We were not 'bald-headed' anymore, and we were starting to look more human again.

We set out in the morning on foot, accompanied by four tired German men, not SS-men, and one SS-woman. Late in the afternoon, before the sun set, we returned to the camp.

Even on the first day we had already taken back a few carrots and radishes – peeled and washed – to give to the girls in the camp. We hid two or three radishes, carrots or small cabbages underneath our aprons. We would ask permission to go to the toilet, and there we would arrange the carrots like ballerinas' whale-bone stays around our waists with our aprons pulled tight so our booty would not fall out.

How pleased we were in the evening when we distributed our vegetables. We took a few at first, and then little by little, becoming more daring, we took more. Our *Kapo* and two or three other girls convinced our SS-woman to let us bring back to the camp the leftover soup and the SS leavings, which were collected to be fed to pigs. I cannot remember where we found the pots and cans to transport the soup in. Many times, when we were not being watched, instead of taking the leftover soup, we would take freshly cooked soup intended for the SS!

In the morning when we set off to work we went quickly. In the evening, though, when returning we shuffled along slowly, as we were loaded down with vegetables. We were becoming more and more daring, and we took more and more vegetables. Throughout the day we were in perpetual motion from the kitchen to the toilet. The carrots were carefully arranged around our waists, and the rest of the vegetables around our ankles.

Naturally all this extra weight made walking awkward. When we sat down to clean vegetables, the different things we had hidden impeded our movements. Our *Kapo* and a couple of others, who worked directly in the kitchen (we worked in a kind of antechamber to the kitchen), were able to take sugar and margarine to bring back to their friends in the camp.

As we walked back to the camp, vegetables would occasionally fall to the ground, as walking made our clothes looser. We just went on walking, pretending that nothing had happened. I am sure the German soldiers knew what we were doing, but they didn't say anything. The SS-woman who accompanied us was always at the front of the line and didn't suspect anything.

We began to load ourselves more and more. My mother borrowed an elastic girdle from one of the girls, I don't know how or where she got it. She promised her a daily 'vegetable ration' if we could use it. Salvation! Now I could arrange lots of stuff around my body. Carrots upright like girdle stays around my body, turnips and celery in my breeches, around which I tightened the elastic more tightly and underneath my breast, cabbage and other things, tightening my apron over them so I would lose nothing. Walking was becoming very difficult with our legs apart, as the vegetables shifted around. Anyway, we all shared the food back in the camp …

Just as with all good things in life, it did not last forever. Our good fortune lasted only 20 days. We were losing vegetables more and more often – given our big loads – and leaving a trail behind us like Hansel and Gretel.

We overdid the whole thing, and one evening when we arrived back at the camp we were stopped outside the gate. 'Inspection,' ordered the SS-woman, 'Come in!' As we stood in a row waiting, we started to jettison everything we had hidden on our bodies and throw it behind us. While we waited for the SS-woman who accompanied us to call the higher authorities of the camp and a few other SS-women, we unloaded all our freight and stood upright at attention, full of self-confidence. An SS-woman started to inspect us, walking slowly in front of us. When she reached the end of the line, she turned to go behind us and ... 'Look here!' she screamed to her colleagues. I also discreetly turned my head, and saw multi-colored heaps of vegetables behind us and some melted packs of margarine in between. 'Had we had carried all this ourselves?' I asked myself with pride! It was mid-April, very close to the end of the month. Despite their wild screams, we were not punished.

Naturally we were never sent back to that *Kommando*, and the next day we were assigned to the 'Wald-Kommando', the forest detachment, as a punishment. We set off very early in the morning, walked for a quarter to half-an-hour and finally arrived at our workplace in the woods.

I remember that on my first day I looked about, admiring and enjoying nature and the landscape. I could feel that it was springtime, little flowers here and there, and on the trees all the buds ready to burst open.

A German forester was waiting for us, not an SS-man. He divided us into pairs, put a log on a saw horse, and we had to cut it down the middle, with each of us pulling on one end of the saw.

The first day it did not seem like a very difficult task. We sawed slowly – nobody forced us to work faster – and chatted among ourselves. For lunch we had a dry piece of bread with nothing on it. They gave us soup in the evening, when we returned.

The fresh air and walking there and back made our stomachs growl with a hunger that became more and more unbearable. It had been good when we worked in the kitchen, it had been good for the girls in the camp too. But now? Our hunger became more and more unbearable. I would bend down to pull out grass stems that had started to grow from the frozen earth. I discovered a herb which was difficult to find but tasted vaguely like onions! Like goats we grazed, trying to satisfy our hunger.

One day in a small stream I found a rotting carrot. Oh! What joy! I removed the rotten part and ate the rest. What hunger, what hunger, my God!

One day, returning to the camp, I found my mother sitting on her bed beside another prisoner, Mrs Cohen, who had become a good friend. She was a Jew from Constantinople and had a pack of cards with her. I don't know how or where she had found it. She knew how to read cards, and everybody was after her to tell their fortune – they would give her a piece of bread or something else to thank her. When I worked in the kitchen, my mother shared whatever I brought to her with the Greek girls and Mrs Cohen.

Mrs Cohen had spread her deck of cards in front of her and was reading them. Both of them were very confused. Mrs Cohen put one card down and said, 'They are dying, there look at this card, it shows there … but then … they don't die.' She dealt the cards again and again, and they showed the same thing. Naturally the people she was talking about were my father and brother. Finally she put the cards away, visibly upset and exhausted, and said: 'Tomorrow we will try again.'

As soon as she woke up the next morning, she read the cards again and, full of joy, she told us, 'They are alive, don't worry. Here, the cards show this.' She dealt the cards and repeated what she had said … I was so affected that I made a mental note of the date, it was 18 or 19 April 1945.

The end of April approached. The Germans were very restless, SS-people came and went, and the guards who accompanied us to our workplace even spoke with us.

Instead of cutting the tree trunks into 80 cm lengths, as we were told to by the forester, we cut 'plates', i.e., slabs of wood about 3 cm thick, which we took back to the camp to use as 'plates'. What would we put on them? It did not matter to us, we wanted plates and we dreamt and thought incessantly of plates full of food. Every plate we cut took the same amount of work as cutting 80 cm lengths, as the forester wanted. This was our passive resistance.

On 1 May 1945 the Germans with their guns ordered us to get ready and form rows of five, as we were to be transferred to another location. They were themselves quite aroused, but they did not stop shouting orders and threatening us: we must keep in line and whoever fell behind would be shot.

The story of January repeated itself, but not with the same cruelty. It wasn't cold, as it was already spring. The SS were not as self-confident as before. They loaded all the camp's documents into a car and we set off. On the way we met other columns, this time of male prisoners.

At a certain point, when we were close enough, I asked some of them where they came from and if they were from Auschwitz. Yes of course, they were from Auschwitz I. 'Did you meet the Kounios?' It was a question I constantly asked when I met male prisoners. Their answer was always the same: 'No, they are not alive, they did not survive the march.' They repeated this with such certainty that little by little we started to believe it, although I still believed deep inside that they really were alive.

Chaos reigned in the streets. Cars full of German civilians carrying their possessions were trying to drive through our lines. Columns of prisoners, some dressed in striped clothes, others in military clothes, were walking, dragging their feet. Where to? Nobody knew.

In all that chaos the Germans often shot and killed prisoners who could not keep up because of weakness. The cannons sounded closer and closer, and the airplanes never stopped flying overhead, but the Germans, faithful to their duties, did not stop killing prisoners until the last minute. Here and there on the side of the road the SS would light a fire and burn files and folders of documents.

Finally we five Greek women decided to steal away and hide in the woods. This woods were teeming with people in hiding. From a distance we could hear trucks passing by, the German's screams, sounds of people and every so often shooting ...

It seemed as though a long time passed as we crouched in hiding. A bit further along were some French soldiers, prisoners of war who had also taken shelter in the woods. We started to talk to them, and they told us that we couldn't stay there, we had to hide someplace. Two of them left to scout the surrounding area. After a long wait they returned looking happy. They had found an abandoned barn where we could hide. We were weakened by hunger and thirst. We were all in bad shape, exhausted and worn. With what joy we followed them! A few more joined us, and we barricaded ourselves in the barn.

The men took turns going out in search of food. They caught three chickens which they brought back triumphantly. Another found a sack of potatoes somewhere. I cannot remember who cooked and how, but I remember very well that for four days and four nights we did not budge from the spot, but ate constantly. After so many weeks of fasting, we ate like kings!

'The Allies or the Russians must be very close,' the French soldiers said. 'Don't worry, we shall soon be liberated.'

On 5 May 1945 the Russians came. In their tanks, camouflaged with twigs attached to their helmets, they rolled closer. I heard my mother saying: 'Like Genghis Khan's hordes!' The Russian soldiers, as we heard later, had been given the order: 'Treat the Germans as they behaved in Russia. Burn, pillage and rape!'

The prisoners-of-war who stayed with us in the barn would not let us go out. The Russians, full of hatred and desire to avenge themselves on the Germans, were destroying everything in their way. They raped any female they happened across – even old women were not spared, one of our comrades told us.

That lasted for 24 hours, and then the regular occupation army arrived. We could breathe freely again, and slowly we started to go out. Turmoil reigned in a small town a bit further on. Prisoners from the camps, weak and hungry, prisoners of war, free foreign workers were all flooding the *Kommandatura* (command posts). The Russian army was trying to impose some order on this chaos, to feed the hungry people, to arrange shelter for them.

We had to change our clothes, to become human again, to find something to cover us at night. 'All the Germans' houses are at your disposal, go in and take anything you need, do as they did to you ...,' a Russian officer told us.

We decided to stay in the barn a bit longer, but also to go in search of the things we needed to make our life a bit more tolerable. I went out together with Esterina to search ... On the way we stopped and watched German refugees, fleeing like hunted animals. They wanted to reach the zones occupied by the Americans and the Allies, because they were not as brutal as the Russians.

Now it was their turn to carry their babies and drag their children behind them. The bewildered women, hair covered by turban-like kerchiefs, were pushing their carts. In many carts sat ill and elderly relatives wrapped in blankets.

They had been sending our people straight to the gas chambers, I thought as I watched a woman bending lovingly over an old man to rearrange a blanket as she pushed the cart. Your turn has come, I thought with immense sorrow.

I asked every freed prisoner I met who had been in Auschwitz about my father and brother. The answer was always the same.

After a while we found ourselves outside a lovely villa, and the wide-open door beckoned to us. I entered reluctantly and found myself in the dining room. The table was set with a snow-white tablecloth, beautiful plates and crystal glasses half-filled with wine. It was obvious that the people had fled in haste. Lost in thought, I contemplated the carefully-laid table and tried to imagine the people who formerly had lived here … And what festive occasion they had been celebrating around such a beautifully set table.

Esterina's voice brought me back to reality and I went upstairs. A huge bedroom with a beautifully made bed and on a night table a picture of an attractive woman with two children in her arms. I reflected on the photograph with mixed feelings and a heavy heart. In front of an open wardrobe Esterina was choosing clothes. I also took what I needed, and also two blankets and a featherbed, and went outside. I could not bear it anymore. On the way back we saw other prisoners, also with loot in their hands. Many of the camp prisoners and prisoners-of-war simply went into houses and after taking what they needed destroyed the furniture and furnishings in a furious rage.

As we left I felt briefly ashamed because of the things we had taken, but our needs were so great that I did not allow myself to think about it.

The Russians were trying to round up all the DPs (displaced persons). A mounted Russian officer rode up to our barn. He spoke broken German. Tall, blond, with blue eyes, he seemed like an ancient God on his horse. He asked us where we were from, and we tried to explain to him. It was easy for him to understand that we were Greeks and Jews, but he couldn't understand, or only vaguely, when we tried to describe our life in the camp. Even when I showed him the number tattooed on my arm he could not grasp what it meant. We were emaciated, with very short hair and very wretched, and that was reason enough for him to want to help us.

He asked if I needed anything, and as I had not been able to find any shoes, I pointed to my feet and said: 'Shoes!' He mounted his horse, gave us a military salute and rode off, not uttering another word. He came back in the afternoon carrying a basket filled with shoes: high-heeled shoes, flat shoes, dance shoes, ballet shoes, boots … white, black, brown, his basket brimming with all kinds of shoes, small, big and many odd pairs. His face was shining with joy, when he saw our pleasure.

He sat down near us and took out a balalaika he had hung over his shoulder. He played for a while, and then he started singing Russian songs in a very beautiful voice. Some people knew the songs and softly sang along with him; we hummed the tunes. I asked him to sing 'Night Bells', the song Vera used to sing to us in Auschwitz. I could hear Vera's crystal-clear voice in my head. Where was she now, I wondered nostalgically. It was an unforgettable evening, full of human warmth!

A few days later the Russians settled us in a barrack where there were very many people, camp prisoners as well as prisoners-of-war. Our aim now was to return to Greece as soon as possible, but we couldn't see how we could manage this. With no documents and no money …

One day four Serbian officers, former prisoners-of-war with whom we had made friends, came to my mother and told her that they were leaving to try to reach the American Occupation Zone. They asked us if we would like to go with them so that we could return to Greece. Naturally we went with them at once.

There were no vehicles, so we started walking. The roads were full of 'all the tribes of Israel', moving in the same direction, and alongside us frightened German refugees fleeing from the Russian Zone of Occupation. As at the Tower of Babel, total confusion prevailed. We moved ahead only very slowly.

When we finally arrived at the American Zone, we went directly to the nearest American command post. Despite the crowds, things were better organized there. We immediately declared that we wanted to go back to our homeland, to Greece. If my father and my brother were still alive, that is where we would meet. For me anyway it was the only place I wanted to go, my beloved hometown.

Esterina, Sarah and Flora did not want to go back, they did

not have anybody waiting for them, all their families had perished. They decided to seek a way to reach Palestine. They had already met some contact people from Palestine and joined them. Jews from Palestine had already organized a transfer center where they prepared anybody who wanted to go to Palestine and settle there.

That is where we parted company, promising each other not to forget and that they would write to us at our Greek address, 15 Venizelou St, Thessaloniki, so that we would know where they were.

The Americans had not yet planned a transport to Greece. The Serbs, however, would be leaving in the next three days. 'Come with us,' Michael Ruszuklic insisted, 'we have a big house and my mother will be delighted to welcome you.'

And so it was. Not quite understanding how, we found ourselves in Belgrade with only the clothes on our backs and one change of underwear. Their house was located in one of the upper-class neighborhoods of Belgrade. Sure enough, Michael's mother welcomed us as if we were family, well-loved family, too! A sparkling-clean room with two beds and snow-white sheets was where we slept. They shared everything with us, although they had very little themselves. After a harsh occupation in which they had lost everything, money was scarce, but their hearts were big and their generosity even bigger.

Michael's younger brother, Galian, also lived in the house. There was an older brother, but they had lost track of him. I was bewildered but trying not to show it. I felt uncomfortable in my unattractive garments, but there was no way to buy new clothes.

I remember one evening when Galian took me out together with two charming cousins. I had washed my dress earlier and cleaned my hair, but I still felt terrible next to the charming Mileva.

I was nineteen, but three years in the concentration camp had not taught me anything that would help me to be a 'charming' girl. When I left Greece I had been a child, and now suddenly I was already a young lady. My years in Auschwitz were still fresh inside me, and I tried constantly to adapt myself to the new environment. Fortunately, I could speak French, so I was able to communicate with them.

One day we went to the most sophisticated establishment in those days – Kale Megdon. Everything was very simple then, but to me it all looked so beautiful! All their friends were there, boys and girls, and they danced and laughed. I did not dare try to dance, as I had no idea how and stayed put in one corner of the room. I was wondering what was I doing together with all these happy people speaking the same language and having fun together. I wanted to leave, to go to Greece, but how?

One young man from the group sat down next to me and started to ask me about my life in Germany. He spoke French and was very interested in the things I was saying. After a while he disappeared and came back carrying a red carnation, which he presented me with! O joy! O beauty!

That is how my first outing in Belgrade went. I never saw the young man with the carnation again. I do not recollect his name, but I shall never forget him!

Meanwhile mother wrote to her cousin in Switzerland and kept looking for a way to get us back to Greece. I helped Michael's mother around the house. She loved showing me things and giving me little hints on cooking. She baked bread once a week. I can still see her in front of me, sleeves rolled up high on her arms, with her sweating, smiling face, kneading and explaining to me how to make the best and tastiest bread! 'And you should know,' she said with a meaningful wink, 'if your bottom isn't sweating, you aren't finished kneading.' Her ingenuity impressed me very much. She could cook the tastiest meals using only the very few ingredients that were available to her. She made the best puddings without eggs or cheese, using only wild herbs which she taught me to pick.

I helped Galian and Mileva work in a potato field. Our job

was to dig up the potatoes and put them in sacks. Our pay was low, but we were allowed to bring home as many potatoes as we could carry.

It was summer, and the sun was shining, the trees were very green, butterflies, bees, birds and colorful wild flowers all around made me feel that I was at a festival. If only I could be sure that my father and brother were alive ... That was always in my mind, together with a terrible pain in my heart.

My memory of Belgrade in those days is that of a gray, ruined town. Shabbily-dressed people, many soldiers in the streets and empty shops. Tito was now in power, and soldiers wore a red star on their army caps. For Michael's family things were not easy, as they were all royalists. But it wasn't any easier for the rest of the people in a country trying to recover from such a terrible occupation.

7 • *A New Life*

Three to four weeks after our arrival in Belgrade an answer came from Switzerland. 'Return home as soon as possible,' my mother's cousin wrote, 'Salvator and Heinz are waiting for you at home.'

The heavens rejoiced, my delight was indescribable, and my impatience to be back home unbearable. The search for a way to reach Greece became more intensive. Michael and his brother went to the railroad station daily to check the schedules.

I had made friends with Mileva and often went to visit her. She sewed her own dresses and made all sorts of things with her deft hands. She made a skirt for me from a thin gray blanket that we had brought back from Germany. I embroidered flowers on it with red wool, and Mileva added a differently colored trim. It was the most beautiful skirt I had ever worn. She sewed a blouse from an old bed sheet to complete my wardrobe. These were the first new garments I had possessed in three years. I felt so happy and was so very grateful to Mileva. They had very little, but they shared everything with us. She wanted me to go back to Greece 'looking decent', as she said. She even tried teaching me to put on make-up.

One day, when we were going on an outing with our little group of friends, I put on my 'new' clothes. Mileva made up my eyes, my lips and my cheeks. We both laughed a lot in the process, and she was really furious when I went to wash myself – I felt like a clown.

How could I ever forget these people, their love, their generosity, their support?

'A train is leaving for Greece in a few days,' Michael told us excitedly one day. It will go as far as the Greek town of Niki outside Florina on the Yugoslavian border. He sent a message to my father – I don't know how he managed it – to let him know when we would be arriving.

We were on a train again, but this time the clickety-clack, clickety-clack was music to my ears. Soon I would see my father and brother again, they were waiting for us. I allowed the passing landscape to draw me back into my memories.

At Niki one of my father's colleagues from Florina, who had been notified in advance, was waiting for us. In those days any travel from one place to another was very difficult, and it was impossible for my father and brother to meet us there. We spent the night in a shabby hotel, not very clean, and the next day we set off for Thessaloniki.

We arrived in the evening. I tried to imagine how my father and brother would look. And there they were in front of us. How thin they looked! But how warmly they embraced us!

Father had found our house in Koromila Street empty and in a bad state, but our beautiful house, even if it was empty, was waiting for us. There were four folding beds, four chairs, one table – just the basics. But it was our old house with its veranda, its garden with white pebbles, facing the sea, the beautiful crystal-clear sea, indigo and turquoise blue, the sea I had dreamed about in the concentration camp. My heart beat joyously like the chiming of a bell, and I wanted to hug and kiss the pebbles, the sea, the sky, the sunset. It did not matter that we had nothing anymore; we were together again, alive, in our house, that was what mattered! My father managed to get his shop back, which was also empty, and he went straight to work.

The clothes, jewelry, linen, the piano that we had entrusted to our acquaintances to look after: everything was gone. Only the living-room furniture, the beautiful carved oak furniture, had been saved for us by Mr Melanidis the photographer, an old friend of my father. All my parents' books in the big bookcase had been kept for us by the Melanidis family, and one day they found their way back into our house. How can a family so decent and honest ever be forgotten?

Together with my father I put the books back on the shelves and caressed them. Everything seemed like a dream, and I tried not to think of the years in the camp. How could I stop thinking back on them, though, when inside I felt that all the people who had died so unfairly were pleading for justice.

I went in search of the houses where my classmates Dorin, May and Rita had lived, but it was as though they no longer existed. Strangers had moved in, and they did not even know who the previous owners were and how their houses had come to be deserted.

How could I not feel the absence of my uncles, my aunts and my cousins – they did not exist anymore. Twenty-three members of our family had perished …

I had to talk about them, to explain to everybody what really happened during those three years. I owed it to those who had died, I owed it to mankind, which had to learn the real story, so that it would not happen again.

I tried to talk, to tell the story – but I could see the denial in people's eyes. They did not want to hear, because they could not believe that what I was saying was true. I could read the doubt in their eyes, they must certainly have thought I had suffered a blow on the head.

Thessaloniki had lost its Jews. Of the few that returned, many left, because they could not bear the loneliness of the town without their relatives. Most of the survivors lived together in houses given to them. Many married quickly, without bringing anything into their marriages except themselves and their memories. They held group marriages, without the joy of being surrounded by their parents, their relatives and their friends. They held hands and, despite all their hopes for happy new lives, cried together because of the absence of their loved ones.

They felt driven to marry quickly to create a new family so they could endure the loneliness and unbearable sorrow.

Many left for Palestine to find a new homeland, and many went to America.

Greece was still struggling to revive its prosperity after the burden of the occupation. The few Jews living in Thessaloniki tried to restore something of the large old Jewish community that had once thrived there. Of the many synagogues in Thessaloniki, the only one that was still able to function was the Monastirioton Synagogue. That is where the weddings were held, and there we all went to celebrate our high holidays.

I started to talk less and less about my concentration camp experiences. Life was going on, I wanted to live, to fill in the gaps, to become one with the people around me. I tried to find my old schoolmates. We were delighted to see each other, we hugged and kissed – but we were so distant from each other. We had each experienced three of the most important years, the adolescent years, in such different ways. Now we had different interests. *Diaplasis* and our club now belonged to the past. My beloved friend Ritza lived in Athens, Roula was married, and so many things came between me and all the other children.

I often got together with my friends Nina Saltiel and her sister Zizi. We shared common recent experiences; they had returned from the terrible concentration camp Bergen-Belsen. Dik Benveniste became part of our group now; he had spent the occupation fighting alongside the partisans in the mountains. There was also the 'blond rider of Koromila Street', Phaedon Kontopoulos, who spent the occupation years in the Middle East, Maria Stangou, my dear friend Alekos Kaldopoulos, Filikos and his wife, a friend who is close to me even today, Nina-Kokkalidou-Nahmia (today a well-known journalist and author), and others …

As we had before the war, we started swimming in the beautiful sea in front of our house. All our old friends and acquaintances from the surrounding neighborhood used to swim in front of our house, Polat's house, Greco's and the

Lycée. We formed our own 'society' in the sea. Nobody imagined that the clean sea would be declared off-limits for swimming a few years later, or that they would fill it in to build a road along the quay.

I tried to find myself, but my concentration camp experiences were so fresh in my memory. My childhood friend and later husband, Rolli Amariglio, gave me much comfort and happiness. He was the first one to visit us after our return, and in the following months we became very good friends. He was then studying at the American Farm School. He was boarding there, and when he had free time he visited us. He taught me how to dance, and together with him and my friends we frequented the 'Friends of the Sea Club'. Sometimes – not too often – we went dancing at the 'Delice', in those days very sophisticated.

On Sundays, together with our friends, we would go up to our 'land', the plot we owned in Arsakli. Our Sunday excursions were among our greatest pleasures. Transportation to Arsakli was very infrequent, and we did not have spare money to spend on taxis. Often we would simply walk there, starting from Martiou Street.

There was little water and no electricity then. We carried our food in rucksacks and off we would go, laughing and giggling towards our 'land' ... We always came back together on foot. The road was deserted, there was rarely a car, and we could walk undisturbed in the middle of the road, chatting and singing.

We used to have many grape-vines then which produced Kapoutsida grapes. My father made wine and 'Tsipouro', a local sort of Ouzo, aided by his assistant, Giorgos Zourelidis, and our 'land' soon became our 'vineyard'.

The vineyard was our joy, not only ours but our friends' too. Along with his welcome to anybody who came there for the first time, my father's motto was: 'Here people do as they wish,' meaning that they should feel at home without observing any formalities.

I went out with Rolli more and more often, and we began to discuss our future. He dreamed of acquiring a smallholding and transforming it into a model farm. He wanted to show the farmers how to get the best results cultivating their land, how to start their own vegetable gardens. I dreamed that I would be a great help to him.

Life was becoming beautiful again and was moving steadily onward. The synagogue started to fill up slowly, and the rabbi blessed the union of many, many young people who, all alone, were trying to recreate their families. Nine months after weddings there would be births and name-giving ceremonies. Every wedding was a mixture of happiness and sorrow, just as all our high holidays were a mixture of joy and tears.

Families were so small then, nearly non-existent. There were no parents, no grandparents, no relatives with whom to celebrate the big events. People were all so lonely!

I could feel so much for them! I have always felt a deep sense of gratitude that I still had my parents and my brother.

A year later, in 1946, the first big celebration was held in our house. My cousin Emilia married Albert Saul. Her wedding took place in our house, because nobody from her family, her four brothers and her parents, had survived. It was a lovely, simple and private wedding; our few friends were all present. 'Your turn now,' people told me – and it wasn't long before my 'turn' really did come.

We held our wedding in June 1947. My father's finances were improving, but he still had no spare money for a dowry and wedding dress. Fortunately, we were getting parcels from the United States, where my father's sister lived. In one of the parcels was a piece of yellow fabric, very beautiful, which we kept so that my mother could sew something for the wedding.

Her health was steadily deteriorating, and she needed an operation to remove her spleen. This kind of operation was difficult in those days, and the doctors gave her a 50 per cent chance of survival. She arranged to have the operation at the Evangelismos hospital in Athens on the 18 June 1947, three days after the wedding. Despite my wish to get married after the operation, she insisted that the wedding should take place first. She was unyielding. Heavy-hearted we started our preparations.

Our seamstress, Mrs Olga Polat, who was both our next-door-neighbor and a friend, sewed our clothes. My father brought 12 bed-sheets from UNRRA (United Nations Relief and Rehabilitation Administration), which had their stamp in one corner, and four blankets. This was my dowry.

Our wedding took place in the synagogue. It was filled with daisies. My father's friend, Mr Markos the florist, took great care to decorate the synagogue as best he could, and the flowers in season were daisies. All our friends gathered to rejoice with us, and the synagogue was full.

My mother was in a bad way. A few days earlier she had become terribly jaundiced because of her illness, and she was thus completely yellow, even the whites of her eyes. She wore the yellow dress made by Mrs Polat and a yellow straw hat – very elegant – she was a symphony in yellow …

Our wedding meal took place at lunch-time in Luxembourg, a local restaurant that is well known to this day, and our honeymoon was in … our house at Arsakli. That is as far as our finances would permit us to go.

One after the other my friends also got married. Zizi married Dik, Nina married Phaedon Kontopoulos and Maria married Alekos Kallidopoulos.

Our dreams of owning a farm fell through. They did not give us the smallholding, and my husband had to do something to feed his little family.

Together with one of his friends he decided to open a shop, the RODAM stationery store, which is still in business today, although it was created on a temporary basis.

The political situation in Greece was not at all good in 1947. The civil war was raging. They started systematically calling up everyone who had not served in the army before. A few months after our wedding Rolli's age group was called up. My husband was away from me: a soldier receiving his basic training in Drama.

Drama is a city in northern Greece, 140 km from Thessaloniki. In those days, with no good roads, it was a long trip – now you can drive there in two hours. Transportation was scarce and we didn't own a private car – a very rare luxury at that time. I decided to visit Rolli in Drama, despite my parents protestations. 'Where will you go, so far away all by yourself without anybody to accompany you?' I decided to go anyway. The 40 days of his basic training would soon be over; who knows where they would send him next? Everything was so insecure and worrisome – but I definitely had to visit him.

Drama really was a 'drama' in those days – a terrible place. It seemed like a big village to me. Our evening outing was to an island where there was a little restaurant. How different from the Drama of today! But nothing was of any importance, as long as I was together with my husband. I stayed with him for two days; they gave him permission to stay out overnight, and then I returned to Thessaloniki via Kavala.

I went to the shop every day; I became a working woman. In those days very few women worked, and when customers from the provinces came to the shop, they looked at me suspiciously ... Things became more serious for me in the shop, because our partner decided to emigrate to America together with his family. Business was difficult in those days, all the goods were imported from abroad. Our faithful clerk, Isaak Masliah, helped me a lot during the years when my husband was away in the army.

Meanwhile, I was learning the job. I remember going to some friends' stationery shop, and I would listen eagerly to what they had to say. I kept my eyes and ears open to listen and learn. I remember that in the early days we used to carry a special brand of 'typewriter paper' which was sold to people from rural areas for use as cigarette paper. They would cut it into small pieces and wrap tobacco in it to make cigarettes. I became an expert at telling which paper was the most suitable. For quite some time we sold reams of 'typewriter paper'.

I would go by tram every day from the Georgiou bus stop to Venizelou Street, a pleasant ride of 20–30 minutes, back and forth four times a day.

I started doing business with the bank. I had to open accounts, pay bills of exchange, borrow money. I remember how anxious I was the first time I went there ... Will I manage? I wondered, and before I entered the bank I would pinch my cheeks to hide the pallor caused by my anxiety. At the concentration camp we used to pinch our cheeks before a selection. The camp was always lurking in my subconscious mind.

One day my brother Heinz gave me a 'diary' to read about his life in the camp, which he wrote as soon as he was back in Greece. Near the end I read his description of how they arrived in the Ebensee camp in Austria:

> On the way to the new camp 20 Russian prisoners escaped. I was impressed by the way they escaped. From the minute they got on the train the Russians never stopped singing. But they weren't singing the songs' real lyrics, they were passing on messages and instructions about how to jump off the cars when it was dark enough at night. The next day the SS immediately realized what had happened, but did not take any action. As soon as we arrived at the camp's rail station, instead of going directly into the camp, they made us wait for a long time and then singled out 20 people. Among them was my father. [According to a letter from Wilibald Pajak to Erika Kounio-Amariglio of 26 February 1996, he likewise arrived in Ebensee on 16/17 April 1945 from Melk.]

My brother did not want to be separated from my father and,

without knowing the purpose of the selection, he asked to join them. Later, when the officer took them to one side, they realized why they had been singled out. Twenty prisoners had been selected for execution as a reprisal for the 20 who escaped. Heinz continued:

> They had set up an execution team, and they all got ready to go to the place of execution. At that moment a junior SS officer came from the Ebensee camp to take over the transport. He asked the SS officer on duty to tell him the number of prisoners he had brought with him. The officer reported that of the 1,400 that he brought with him, 20 had been separated and made to stand on the side, because they were going to be executed. A discussion began between the two SS officers. The junior officer from the camp said that he should have executed them at once when he noticed that 20 persons had escaped. Now nothing could be done. They had to be brought into the camp as usual, and then they would see … The junior officer hurried off towards the camp very excitedly. The SS officer who had accompanied them ordered the 20 men to continue on to the place of execution. They walked slowly despite beatings and SS goading. After a while the junior officer reappeared bringing an order that they [the 20] first had to be properly registered in the camp and after that executed, and he led them all into the camp. (Details from Heinz Salvator Kounio's book (in Greek), *I Experienced Death*, Thessaloniki, 1982, pp. 138–42, here p. 172.)

As I read this description, my memory of Mrs Cohen in the Malchov camp came back to me with the speed of a lightning bolt. I could see her confused face in front of me, saying: 'They are dying, but no they are not dying …'

I looked at the date, it was 17 April 1945. Almost the very same date was etched in my memory, this was 18 April, the next day, when Mrs Cohen said: 'They are living, don't worry.' What a coincidence, what an omen! We talked about it for days after that, and I could not get it out of my mind.

The days went by. One day followed the other, filled with the thousands of things we had to do in order to get back on our feet.

My husband was now serving in Kozani. Fortunately not on the front line. He was already an 'old' married man! Small things bring everything to the surface again. For example, one time I was looking for fabric to make a summer dress, and the salesperson brought a roll of silk fabric, blue with white polka dots. Immediately I remembered the dresses we wore in the camp. I react the same way to striped patterns.

I never allowed myself to go hungry again. Despite my wish to stay thin, I didn't want to go on a diet. My refrigerator was always full, and bread was never lacking in my household. I refused to be upset about unimportant things, for instance when a dress didn't come out like I wanted it to or a crystal vase broke or … Everything was so meaningless compared with the most important fact – that we were all four of us alive.

The year 1949 brought with it the end of the civil war. Greece breathed a sigh of relief. After all, we were all the same, we were all brothers, but passions were still smoldering underground. In 1950 my husband was still serving in the army. Now a new worry, there was a war raging in Korea. They would send troops from Greece. Would they send him too? Again he was lucky, because he was an 'old' married man!

The year 1950 was very important for me. I became pregnant. On 9 April 1951 our son Errikos-Riki, was born. Exactly ten years before, on 9 April 1941, the Germans had entered Thessaloniki. In my mind the past and the present coexist.

I remember that one day I laid my baby on the table after his bath and played with him, kissing his tummy. I was listening to his cooing laughter and his little legs and arms were kicking the air… Without wanting to, I remembered the concentration camp. That horrible summer of 1944 when tens of thousands of Jews arrived daily from Hungary. The crematoria had too little capacity, and so they dug big pits. Together with the corpses they were throwing live babies, infants, little children up to two years old into the flaming pits. Which means, I thought to myself, that this little child, my baby, would have been thrown into the flames too … How could it be possible? The picture was ever present in my mind, and as my son grew, I would think: 'even now that he is a year old they would still have thrown him into the pit.'

I tried very hard not to think of it, but every so often when he started to crawl and to stand up, the same picture continued to come back into my mind. And gradually I came to understand more and more the enormity of Germany's crime: the brutality, the systematic planning for the extermination of the Jews.

One more picture would come into my mind then, that of the camp director, whose villa was very close to our office, on the other side of the barbed wire. He used to live there together with his wife, his beautiful Gretchen and their four or five children … Small, beautiful, fair-haired children whom he used to play with when he came home from the camp – after watching small, beautiful, dark-haired children being burned in the fires …

In the meantime, my husband was finally discharged. Our little boy grew in our little house at 4 Filellinon Street, and on 4 April 1953 our daughter Theresa was born. Their grandfather and grandmother were just as excited as we were about their grandchildren.

In 1965 the first International Conference of the Survivors of Auschwitz was held in Warsaw. Together, my mother and I represented the Jewish deportees from Thessaloniki. The conference in Warsaw lasted for two days, and its motto was **NEVER AGAIN**.

Erika's mother Hella Kounio, 1953.

The purpose was to discuss the best ways to inform and awaken the world so that such a terrible thing would never be repeated. The conference delegates came from more than 30 different countries from the East and West blocs. Besides Europe, survivors were present who lived in America, Argentina, Israel, Brazil and Australia. We held our discussion united in brotherhood around a big table.

Erika's father, Salvator Kounio, 1953.

During the breaks I tried to speak with other participants to find out details of how they had been brought to the camps. Most of them had long stories to tell. Paul Halter from Belgium had fought in Spain and like many others was active in the resistance before being arrested. A Frenchman had served with the 'Maquis', the French resistance movement.

Five Christian Germans had been caught very early on and were dragged from one camp to the next for resisting Hitler's policies. It was the same with an Italian and, of course, the Poles. Many of the people present had created a nucleus of resistance active inside the camp.

I kept on asking and listening ... As if I were still hidden in the cabinet of our office in the camp, reading their files with the history of their activities and arrests. I wondered, after a while – what am I doing among these very special people? They were active, they risked their lives many times for a purpose, and the price they paid was to be caught and imprisoned. They knew why they had been sent to the camps. What was I doing among them. I hadn't done anything similar. They took me away like a sheep, and I did nothing. I felt so humiliated.

After the conference they gave us a tour around Warsaw, to the ghetto where the Jews had resisted and with improvised bombs, Molotov cocktails, gasoline in bottles, had managed to keep the Germans at bay for days.

Then we went to Cracow, and the final event of the conference was a visit to the Auschwitz concentration camp. We set off towards Auschwitz by rail. The trip was long, and we filled many coaches. The relatives of many of the delegates accompanied us. How different it was! I had the opportunity to listen and hear the stories of some of the other survivors. They each had a different story with the same ending: all ended in the camp.

Half of the delegates were from the Eastern bloc – 'communists' – nevertheless in the course of several days we were all joined in brotherhood with no difference in our views, all respectful of and loving towards one another.

It grew dark, and after our long conversations we all retreated silently into our own private thoughts. Suddenly from the silence of the night, accompanied by the train's clickety-clack, clickety-clack, somebody began to sing a very sad, charming Russian song. When he stopped, without any prompting an Italian sang an Italian ballad, then a Serb, again a Russian, a Pole, and we all burst into highly emotional applause. Then somebody turned to us and said we should sing something familiar from our country. My mother and I sang 'The Pireus Children' (from *Never on a Sunday*), and enthusiastically they all hummed along with us; some sang in their own language. It was such a powerful emotion that we all felt completely united! The last song was begun by two Russians and a Pole; it was 'Night Bells'. We all hummed along quietly with them. Vera came back to my mind … Where was she now? Why do passion and hatred separate people? What did the East and West blocs stand for? I wondered.

The next day we got off the train on the same platform as in 1943!

How quiet it was. Was it possible that I was here again?

First we went to Birkenau. I went off to the side and walked by myself … There was Block 26, where we slept, there were the offices, the latrines, there was Block 25, where the condemned were held … How quiet. My God, how quiet. But in my ears I could hear the lamenting, the screams of pain, the prayers, the howls of the dogs, the 'barking' of the SS.

It was the souls of the dead who were wandering, I told myself … The sun was bright, but I could see shadows everywhere. Shadows of all the people who had perished. I walked along, and there was no mud or snow. My heart felt tighter and tighter.

For the first time I could see the gas chambers and the crematoria close-up. It seemed that there were voices crying out of the smokestacks. It seemed unbelievable to me that all that had happened. There was a place with ashes and bones outside.

They were looking for me; they were calling me. We left for the main Auschwitz camp. We passed under the gate with the inscription: '*Arbeit Macht Frei*' (work makes you free).

All the blocks, buildings, undisturbed in their neat rows as if nothing had happened. There was Block 1, where my father and brother worked. It was on those steps that he would stand so I could see him …

We entered the Auschwitz museum. I stood speechless in front of an enormous pile of shoes. So many thousands, children's, men's, women's. Another big pile, this one of spectacles, so many, so many. A bit further on a pile of artificial limbs – something I found difficult to conceive of – were there so many disabled people? Another big pile attracted my attention. It was full of toys, dolls and other children's things, and further on a pile of hair cuttings which the Germans had not had time to use: blonde plaits, brunette, black hair, curls, hair, hair and more hair… Could that have been Rita's braids? I could not take it any more. I burst into tears.

The Auschwitz concentration camp is a monument to remind humanity for ever that there once was a nation full of clever, educated, hard-working, disciplined and methodical people … And that these people planned and put into effect the 'Final Solution': the plan to systematically eliminate from the face of the earth a whole people, with the sole excuse that they were of a different 'race' and had different beliefs. They believed in the same God their ancestors had believed in and their ancestors before them, who all belonged to a religion from which the religion of Christianity arose … And in the name of this difference they had committed the biggest crime in all the history of our civilization.

Often I am tortured by the thought, why did I survive and not May or Dorin or Rita? What fate separated us and why? Was it all just a coincidence?

Was it just a coincidence that we found ourselves in the first transport, and among 2,800 people we were the only ones who spoke German?

Was it just a coincidence that we were assigned to work in the Political Department the whole time we were imprisoned in Auschwitz?

Was it a coincidence that although both my mother and I came down with typhoid fever, they did not send us to the gas chamber?

Was it just a coincidence that we held out when so many couldn't survive the long march, the cold, the hardship, the hunger, the bleeding, frozen feet?

Erika Amariglio with her husband Rudolf and their family, 1993.

Was it just a coincidence that I worked in the SS kitchen and in this way survived the terrible hunger that devastated the camp?

These are questions that will stay forever unanswered in my mind.

Fifty years later the only answer I can think of is that everything was a coincidence. We were saved by coincidence.

I never forget my profound sense of gratitude for our having been liberated and reunited with my father and brother.

In spite of all the Germans could do, we survived!

Today I have seven grandchildren: Lior, Iris, Tomer and Omri, Charles, Erika and David.

For my grandchildren and all the children of the world of any religion, I have written my testimony 50 years later so that they will be able to reply to anyone who dares to deny there was a Holocaust and so that they will always be on guard to make sure that there will never again be another Holocaust:

NEVER AGAIN

Epilogue

The first edition of my book was published in Greece in April 1995. Two or three weeks after this we were at the synagogue at a memorial service for all the Jews who perished in the gas chambers or died from hardship in the Nazi concentration camps. The synagogue was crowded for the service, as it is every year, and it took me a long time to get out. Shelley Cohen, the community secretary, was waiting for me. 'Where were you?' she said, 'I was looking for you everywhere…' I looked at her in surprise as she went on; 'This lady has been looking for you all morning.' I had hardly opened my mouth to answer her when the lady, eyes full of tears, took my hand into hers and said: 'I must talk to you…'

I couldn't hear a thing, as people were moving and talking all around us. I took the lady by the hand and we went back into the synagogue that was now almost empty. As we sat down she started talking to me obviously very deeply moved. 'In 1943 I was ten years old and I used to live right next door to you in Makedonias Street. One day towards the end of March 1943, after you had left the house to go to the camp, I was playing in your garden when two big lorries stopped in front of your empty house. Full of curiosity, I climbed on top of the fence in order to watch these men who came out of the trucks and went in and out of the house, carrying furniture, mattresses and boxes stuffed with things. They were loading everything into the trucks. I sat glued to the fence as I did not want to miss anything that was going on. After a while they seemed to have got everything they wanted. Then one man approached me and gave me two little toys. "Here you are little one, something for you to play with," he said. When I read the book a few days ago, I was convinced that the toys were yours…'

As she bent over her open handbag, I could see my book inside it with many pages underlined with an orange marker.

She took out something wrapped in foil. 'This belongs to you,' she said, 'I looked after it very carefully all these years.' I unwrapped the foil. 'Oh! This is my little barrel! My brother had the same toy in the shape of a cube!' It was a small wooden puzzle barrel that you could take to pieces and put back together. 'Yes,' she said, 'They gave me the cube as well, but I do not know what happened to it.' By now we were both crying on each others arms. 'Please tell me what's your name?' I asked her. 'Katie…' she said. In that emotion-filled moment I could not recall her surname and when she stopped talking she disappeared into the crowd, leaving me sitting there holding the little barrel in my hands.

I could not find Katie anywhere. I went to Makedonias Street where her house used to be. Now there is a block of apartments in its place. I asked if they knew Katie but the response was negative, as it was up and down the street. A friend promised me to find her but to no avail. I talked to my family and friends about Katie. I described her as best I could. She was not too tall, a brunette with a very sweet face. I began to wonder if I would recognise her if I met her again or passed her on the street. I kept on telling the story to everyone hoping that somebody would recognise who she was.

Two years later, I received a telephone call from my brother who said; 'I have found the Katie you were looking for. I met her daughter who works at my doctor's and she gave me Katie's address and telephone number.' I called her immediately to invite her over my house. I cannot describe my happiness and my emotion when she came over with her daughter and grand-daughter.

Today I often think of Katie, and in my mind's eye she always appears as the little girl on top of the fence watching everything around her with wide eyes. This little girl, a witness of one of the darkest periods of our century, kept this wooden toy out of respect and in memory of this incident. The little wooden barrel has a special place among my precious souvenirs. When I tell Katie's story I often hold it in my hands.

Thank you Katie.